FROM UTOPIA
TO THE
AMERICAN DREAM

JOHN CZINGULA

John Czingula/From Utopia to the American Dream
Printed in the United States of America

From Utopia to the American Dream/ John Czingula -- 1st ed.

ISBN 9781794898639 Print Edition

I dedicate this book to two wonderful people, my parents Dezso Czingula and lren Czingula, who dedicated and sacrificed their lives to bring me and my siblings up through incredible hardship, during and after the Second World War in Europe followed by the dungeons of darkness with the Soviet occupation and communism in Hungary.
I did not realize as a small child and teenager the enormous sacrifice they had endured for us. Not until I came to the United States as a refugee after the revolution of 1956 and could compare life here and what my parents went through to make sure we survived those inhumane days and know the truth. As children we thought that's life, that's how it has to be. But as my Father and Mother would teach us, back then-that's not how it has to be! God bless them. I shall never forget them.

LAND OF MILK AND HONEY
1937–1940

In the peaceful, carefree days before the war, we lived on the outskirts of Szerencs, Hungary. Szerencs was a picturesque sugar and chocolate factory town of 35,000, which smelled of roasting hazelnuts. My parents, Deszo and Irén, had the biggest house in Fecskes Telep or Swallow Camp, a tiny two-street community filled with great people. I was born in that house on March 23rd, 1937, just like my older sister, also named Irén, a few years earlier.

Although I was a very small boy, I have memories of a large foyer, a big well-tended garden, and a back gate that led to golden fields of corn and sunflower. Snow-capped mountains rose in the distance. There was a tree I loved to climb, which bore little green peaches. Lilacs lined the front of the house. The nearby reservoir was filled with clear water and rainbow trout. It fed the factory and the town's beautiful tiled public mineral baths.

My most vivid memories of those carefree early years were of the days I spent at play with my friends Kondas Tibi and Muhi Jancsi on the two streets with the köz or connection in the middle. No one had cars, so we ran back and forth, in and out of each other's houses, stopping in at the Csernyak neighborhood grocery— no bigger than a kitchen—where the owner gave us sour cherry candy. We spent hours rolling old bicycle wheels up and down the streets with sticks. Most of our fathers worked for the railroad and we were all everyone's kids. We were always welcome at neighbors' like the Megyeris.

I have memories of watching my mother, a trained hairdresser, style the hair of the sugar and chocolate executive's wives. I loved taking early morning walks with my grandfather to the nearby village of Mezozambor to get fresh milk and I'll never forget the Chinese porcelain set my parents bought—delivered in a laundry basket by two Orthodox Jewish brothers complete with beards, hats, and long sideburns. I was so surprised by their appearance, I apparently said, "I'm going to faint right here."

It was a statement my parents never let me forget!

There were precious few dangers in those innocent days. We were told to stay out of Takta creek with its ice-cold rushing water and tangles of algae, although we still jumped in sometimes. There was a rumor of a mysterious underground tunnel running nearly twenty kilometers from a nearby castle, which had been built in the 1500s. Parents warned their kids to keep out of this tunnel because it was ancient and could easily collapse. Legends say the tunnel started in the Rákóczi castle in Szerencs. The Turks occupied a large part of Hungary and the Balkans for over a hundred years until the siege of Nándorfehérvár on July 22, 1456, led by Hunyadi János, the Count of Temes and captain general of Hungary. It is now called Belgrade. The battle stabilized the southern frontiers of the_Kingdom of Hungary, delayed the Ottoman advance in Europe, and was celebrated by the Pope who ordered all Catholic church bells to ring at noon, which they still do today.

Along with staying away from these famous tunnels, we were also told to stay off the railroad tracks, which, for me, was the most difficult warning of all. I was obsessed with trains. I loved the railyard and often asked my father, who ran the railroad greenhouse garden, to take me there so I could watch the huge steam locomotives which seemed like fairytale giant serpents to be slain or tamed.

The railroad ran in my blood. On my father's side, all the men going back to the late 1800s were railroad men. Even my older sister worked for the railroad before she got married.

My grandfather Janos—after whom I am named—was a stationmaster. In those days, before the war, especially in the early 1900s, it was a very respectable and responsible job. All the men had nice-looking uniforms and were ranked like the military. They saluted each other and were serious about what was considered to be a lifetime occupation.

My grandfather oversaw permitting or denying trains entrance into the railroad station. It depended, of course, on how busy the rails were and whether a given rail line into the station was free for the approaching train. He did this job by working the railway semaphore signals. The semaphore system involved pivoted arms which signaled the train drivers. Grandfather controlled the semaphores outside the station by pulling large levers in his tower. These levers, through a series of wires and pulleys, would work semaphores outside of the station, sometimes quite far away. If the semaphore—at the top of a tall metal pole—was pointing up at 45 degrees, then the train could proceed into the station. If it was in a horizontal position, the train needed to stop.

My father also came to hold an important position with the railroad, and was a very hard working and diplomatic gentleman, but was apparently something of a rebel in his teens. On one occasion, he and his buddy decided to find out how the semaphore worked by climbing up the metal pole to investigate. Little did they know there was a train approaching.

When my grandfather pulled the lever to signal it was safe to enter the station without stopping, my father was caught and squeezed in the arm of the semaphore, preventing it from raising to the correct 45-degree position. Instead of continuing into the station, the engineer stopped his train.

Of course, this was a complete disaster for my grandfather, especially when he found out his very own son had caused this stoppage. By the time the railroad men dismantled some of the parts, got my father down from the top of the pole, and the train could proceed into the station, it was forty-five minutes late. This almost ended my grandfather's career. He was put before the equivalent of a military tribunal—a railroad court martial—and nearly lost his prestigious job and rank.

For the first time, my father was severely punished. This was a profound and significant turn of events in his young life. Because of this shame, my father left home. He had no money, no trade, craft, or profession. He didn't know what to do. Because it was the beginning of World War I, he lied about his age and enlisted in the Hungarian army.

They soon discovered he was underage, but he was already in uniform and undergoing basic training. Instead of discharging him, they assigned him to a hospital train as an assistant to the medical team. His main task there was to carry severed limbs up front to the steam engine to be burned in the fire box. He told us many years later the difficulty of his job made him a man and changed him forever.

When the war was over, my father did not return home. Instead, he traveled from eastern to western Europe doing odd jobs to survive. When he found work in a large facility where they grew all kinds of plants, trees, and flowers, he realized he had found his calling. He stopped drifting, went to school, and got a degree in horticulture.

My father was twenty-six when he finally returned to Hungary, a grown man with a unique skillset. He reunited with my grandfather who was not only proud of what his son had become but led him toward a lucky professional break.

The Hungarian railroad had multiple large horticulture establishments with different locations across the country where they grew trees, flowers, and designed parks around the railroad stations. They actually planted fruit trees along the railroad tracks and allowed the fruit to be picked for free by the local people in the region. Each horticulture establishment had two or three hundred people working for them.

My father continued the family tradition by becoming a manager and ranking official, uniform and all, when he was hired to run one of the large railroad horticultural establishments. He oversaw hundreds, and managed many greenhouses, laboratories, and park designs.

I loved my handy, intelligent, father and my tall, white-haired grandfather with the bushy mustache. To me, they were the epitome of all that was good. Because they both worked for the railroad, that became my ultimate career goal as well.

One of them anyway . . .

SOMETHING IN THE AIR

My father was sent to Hatvan to run the railroad horticultural center in 1940. Hatvan was a fairly large town with an incredible engine-house facility, and we lived near the railyard in Zsolca, a community of row houses occupied by other families of the railroad.

My father had an office in a building separate from the greenhouse garden complex which featured an aquarium he built himself. I was very proud of him, especially when Horthy Istvan— a fighter pilot, high-ranking Hungarian air force officer, and the son of Admiral Horthy Miklos the Governor of Hungary—came to visit the railroad gardens. I wanted to be a fighter pilot too when I saw Horthy's entourage pull into the railroad gardens in an ultra-modern diesel train engine built into the two-car system.

The news went around the whole of Hatvan and a lot of people crowded the overpass atop the rails to see this famous dignitary. On this special day, my mother went into labor with my younger brother. Horthy Istvan was standing beside my father when he received the news that my mother had given birth to a healthy son. He asked if he could be the godfather.

That is how my new brother came to be christened Istvan.

It was an honor, which was all the more poignant when Istvan Horthy's fighter plane stalled and crashed shortly after takeoff one year later in Russia on August 20, 1942. His father had resisted the Germans up to that point, but after the death of his son the president capitulated to their demands.

Hungary would soon be overrun with Germans.

During those last days in Hatvan, I have many happy memories starting with Istvan as a baby. On hot days, my mother would put him in a large white dish filled with water. As he sat there, his legs were as round as the curvature of the dish.

I thought it was cool, but my mother was worried he had a deformity. Our neighbor, Mrs. Jokai, tried to console her by saying, "My legs were like that and see how they straightened out."

Her legs were just as crooked in her old age as my brother's, which, thankfully, straightened out when he began to walk.

I had good friends in Hatvan including Henter Joska, Macska Jancsi, and others. We played on a playground that had several bicycles with wheels but no tires, all welded together on a single round rail. My father built us a swing for our yard. He also made us a sled for the winter.

Our neighbor, Jokai Neni, had two sons who were both locomotive engineers. They were my heroes, and I always ran out to greet them when they came home with their oily, sooty faces.

I remember when my father and two other friends went to a nearby village to get potatoes for the winter. They came home drunk, singing all the way home. My sister and I had never seen him drunk.

One of Dad's friends raised rabbits. My mother wanted to cook a rabbit he brought home to live in a sack. He hooked the sack up on a tree branch and hit the sack until the rabbit didn't move. When he took it out, skinned it, and handed it to my mother, I was more amazed than repulsed. We didn't have refrigeration back then, and it was just the way things were done.

I was less nonplussed when my mother put a dishwater dish on the stove, lit the fire, and went somewhere saying, "When I come back it'll be nice and warm, and I'll wash the dishes."

We had a canary at the time that my sister let out of the cage. We both watched in horror as the canary landed in the water, began to clean her wings, and promptly died.

That Christmas, my sister and I got a stuffed clown doll. We were playing with it outside, close to the street door in our yard. We left it there and it disappeared.

"The gypsies opened the street door and stole it," my mother said.

My sister and I also got a tricycle. She jumped onto the seat from the green kitchen chair and the big front wheel and steering arms broke off. Grandpa fixed it by nailing a piece of wood under the seat.

Henter Joska and I made a plan to see the world by pulling each other around on it, agreeing that I'd pull him until I got tired, then he'd pull me, and vice versa. We set off toward Budapest—that was until it started to get dark, at which point we were both panicked and hungry, and decided to abandon our plan.

Because we shared a fence and one of the pieces was nailed down only at the top, we would push it over to the side and go back and forth between each other's yards planning out our next adventures like the Hungarian version of Tom Sawyer and Huck Finn.

We moved on to catching sparrows and making soup out of them at Macska Jancsi's house. He lived across the street and was an older and wiser ten years old. Wiser than I was, especially after I jumped off the swing and landed on a broken bottle with my bare foot.

My parents were not home that day, so Grandpa Janos ripped a bed sheet apart and wrapped it around the wound, which was deep and bleeding profusely. He put me on his back and ran all the way to the doctor's office as I sobbed my eyes out. The bedsheet was soaked with blood before we ever got there.

It wouldn't be my last injury, even that year. By summer, I would be hurt again when Macska Jacsi, Henter Joska, my sister, and I were eating peach seeds. We would put the large outer seeds on a tree stump and break them open with a small axe so we could eat the delicious, dried seeds inside. When my turn came, I slipped, the axe turned in my hand, and I cut my foot right between the big toe and the next toe.

I have the scar to this day.

Three houses down lived a nice little girl my age. I had been thinking about her a lot and was hoping she was in her yard so I could get a good look at her.

As I was walking by, there she was, dancing!

She looked at me as though she'd been waiting for me too! She said nothing but walked over to some dried flowers in her garden, took the beer bottle cap that happened to be in her hands, and scooped some seeds into it. Silently, she handed them to me through the fence.

It was the beginning of my first love affair.

I brought her a flower and other little gifts from our yard. We longed to play together but her parents wouldn't let her outside her yard.

I didn't realize why at the time, but the war had already started.

One afternoon, I was walking with my mother and sister, in down-town Hatvan. As we neared the church, we saw a group of people working on the lawn. All had yellow stars on their chests. Several black uniformed men threatened them with sticks, hitting some of them to make them work faster. I'd heard the word *Jew* from my experience with the Hasidic brothers who'd come to our house outside of Szerencs but did not know what was going on or understand their predicament.

I was looking back and fell down.

A soldier who happened to be walking next to me stepped on my left hand, crushing my little finger.

He didn't stop or apologize.

Little did we know how much more there would be to apologize for, and how soon.

THE BACKGROUND MUSIC OF WAR
1943–1944

I was five years old when my father was transferred again, this time to Debrecen to run the railroad garden operation there. My grandparents on my mom's side had a farm on the outskirts of town. It was my grandmother's dream to have my mother and her grandchildren close by, but she also had an ulterior motive— with my father's talent and the manpower of our family, she could now develop their five-acre farm into a flower and vegetable producing enterprise.

Of course, my mother was happy to be with her mother in the city where she was born. Debrecen is the capital of Hungary's Northern Great Plain region. Its two-towered, nineteenth-century Reformed church sits on the expansive main square, Kossuth Tér. Hungary's largest Calvinist Church is situated in Debrecen, so the city is sometimes known as "Calvinist Rome." The Great Calvinist Church of Debrecen was built in 1805 over the ruins of the former church that had been ravaged by fire in 1802. That church was built upon the site where various churches had existed since the 1300s. Hungary's independence was declared in the church on April 14, 1849, when Lajos Kossuth was chosen as the governor/president within the walls of the church.

My parents were happy to settle in Debrecen, and the farm life was theoretically an ideal place for a boy like me, even if it was a bit lonely at first. I made do with chickens, a rooster, geese, pigs, and a dog for companionship and a new school to look forward to.

Our farm kitchen had a large table in the middle that seated all seven of us. On one side we had an old woodstove. It also burned coal, which was hard to come by, smelly, and dangerous because of the carbon monoxide emissions. The other side of the kitchen had a large credenza with all the plates, dishes, baking equipment, and utensils. Beside the credenza was a door to the pantry where we kept all the food that didn't have to be in the bunker for the winter: flour, sugar, lard, smoked meat, bacon slabs, sausages, and honey. To the left and right of the kitchens were the bedrooms. It was small for seven people, eight when my other grandpa came for a visit, but we made do.

At first, I found my grandmother on my mom's side curt and rude. My other grandfather was nice but distant. An intelligent man, he'd been an executive in a large tobacco factory in Debrecen but retired because he'd become very forgetful. He spoke seven languages but had started to mix them up. He'd been a Russian prisoner of war for seven years after the First World War and had suffered a brain injury, so it was assumed he was mentally ill as a result. In truth, he was suffering from Alzheimer's disease.

He was childlike and very docile, and Grandma called him crazy and pushed him around roughly. I knew she was the twelfth child in the Biri family and must have had a tough childhood, but I still hated to see her treat him so badly.

She would soon prove to be the toughest and most valuable member of our family.

I had just started first grade in 1943 at Csapókert school when the Germans took over Hungary.

I'd been in school just long enough for my mother to volunteer me to recite poetry at a beginning-of-the-year event, when we were told we would not be attending for a while. I wondered why we needed to stay home. The Germans had already occupied most of the large buildings and schools across the country, and there had been no resistance. Not a single shot had been fired.

To me, the German soldiers weren't so much dangerous as awe inspiring in their impressive uniforms with their side-holstered guns. They gave chocolates and candy to us kids. They also had beautiful German shepherd dogs. Although, one day, there was a young German soldier walking some officer's German shepard. I was about to pet the dog, when the soldier commanded him to snarl and bark at me. At the sight of his teeth and the sound of his vicious howl, I jumped back and fell into a ditch, splitting my thigh open against a sharp brick. As I lay there bleeding, the soldier and his dog walked on like nothing had happened.

I still bear the scar from that incident to this day.

And then the bombings from the Allied forces began to scar the countryside all around me . . .

My father dug a bunker a safe distance from the house in a nearby field. It was twenty-four feet long, five feet wide, and seven feet deep.

He covered it with railroad ties and placed a layer of earth on top of the ties. While we had to run a bit of a distance to get there, we felt relatively safe from air raids in our earthen bunker. I liked it there because it was nice and cool in the summer, but it was tight with the entire family huddled inside.

When there was enough advance warning, we also went to my great uncle's farm, way out in the country. The village closest to his farm was called Bánk. Large shallow bunkers were built to accommodate the many people who'd fled there as well. Unlike my grandma, my uncle Mihály was kind by nature and took in anyone who asked to be let in from the city.

One night, we all watched what looked like fireworks from the relative safety of his farm on the hill as the largest targets in the city were bombed. First, the Debrecen railroad station and rails were destroyed, including my father's railroad gardens, then the railroad wagon manufacturing plant, and on it went . . .

Once the bombing raid was over, we went back to our home traumatized, but thought since they'd destroyed the largest targets in the city, we were fairly safe.

The American, English, and Russian Allies were relentless against the Germans as they pressed forth to invade Russia. Meanwhile, the Germans used our Hungarian Army at the front in their quest for domination. Thousands of Hungarian soldiers died fronting the Germans.

As the bombings continued, we started to recognize the different fighter planes and insignias, not only of the Germans, but of the

American, English, and Russian Air Forces as well. My favorite was the American P51—it was beautiful, shiny, graceful, and the fastest of all. Not only did it make a serious sound, but it was also always in command of the sky. The P51 was always the last one to disengage from a fight, unlike the Russian fighter planes, which were the first to depart battles. My father said they didn't carry enough fuel. The German 109s, with swastikas on their wings, made a shrieking sound as they dove toward the ground to escape their opponent's bullets or attacked tanks, heavy artillery, trains, and concentrations of soldiers.

One sunny afternoon, with no air raid siren to warn us, one of the enormous German bombers my brother and I called *The Giant* flew extremely low, trailing black smoke from two of its six engines. Sinking steadily toward the ground, the bomber plane managed to fly almost out of sight. Then, we heard the crash and witnessed the spectacular explosion.

In the late summer of 1944, the sirens started up and the usual panic ensued. We all dropped everything as my mother shouted to my father, "Get the children and run for the bunker."

My sister was always first. My father and brother were always next, and mother would always be the last to start running. She had to make sure we were all on our way, everything was off the stove, and the doors to the house were locked so no one could come in and steal anything. We'd heard stories from neighbors about this happening on a regular basis.

As for me, I often pretended to wait for my mother because it gave me time to gaze up at the fighter planes. While we'd always made it to the bunker in time, on this day my father whisked my brother into his arms—he was four at the time—grabbed my hand, and off we went running to the bunker. I could not keep up, so he let go of my hand and ran ahead of me with my brother, all the while yelling, "Run! Run! Run!"

I could also hear my mother's voice in the distance behind us. "The airplanes are coming!"

I was looking up to the sky when Father and Mother yelled from either direction, "Get down! Now!"

I watched Father throw himself on the ground into our carnation field and cover my little brother with his body. I threw myself down too but turned onto my back hoping to see airplanes. Sure enough, a Russian fighter plane had broken off from the others and was diving towards us, guns blazing.

Puffs of dirt flew up beside me and headed toward my father as one of the fighter planes sped by maybe thirty feet above us. I could clearly see the red star on the plane's tail as it pointed back up, re-engaged in the fight, and maneuvered in and around the battle. I was scared but fascinated by these wondrous machines flying in every direction, their slick bodies shining in the sun.

Even though one burst into flames and another started smoking, I thought to myself, "I'd like to do that someday."

Then, as quickly as it started, the planes disengaged and disappeared into the clear blue sky. I looked toward where my father and brother lay in the carnation field and saw no movement. My heart was cold with terror until, a few seconds later, he got up and began running toward the bunker.

"Thank God!" my mother shouted. "Where is Jonny? Oh, my God! I can't see him."

I was there lying on my back trying to process what was going on all around me when my mother yanked me up from amongst the carnations. "Thank God you are alright."

"Follow me!" Father shouted.

We all made it safely to my sister in the bunker. With the sound of the sirens signaling the raid was over and we were out of danger, we hugged and clung to each other.

Mother kept saying, "Next time we hear the sirens we have to run right away. Do you understand?" Then she cried out, "Look at your pants!" pointing to my father's trouser leg. "Are you hurt? Are you bleeding? Why aren't you bleeding?"

"What's wrong? Why would I be?" he asked, looking completely confused.

Mother pointed to three bullet holes in Father's right pant leg. Amazingly, when he'd thrown himself to the ground in the carnation field, his pant leg had spread out and had been pierced by three bullets from the Russian fighter plane. All three shots had missed him by centimeters.

A true miracle!

My brother and I spent weeks searching for those bullets but never found them. Despite it all, I was enchanted by the magnificent planes that flew overhead, and no longer wanted to be a railroad engineer like I'd planned, but a fighter pilot who flew the American P51.

Other than the dog fights and the ever-present threat of a bombing, life went on. My parents and their friends spoke incautious, hushed tones about the Germans losing and all the Hungarian soldiers who had already died on the Russian front. A lot of talk centered around the battle at the Don River and that if the Russians invaded Hungary, it would be the end of the world. Everyone knew the Russians had sent 200,000 men to help the Austrians when the Hungarians were trying to break off from the Austro-Hungarian Empire in 1848. The Russians were barbaric and feared by all. Everyone prayed for the Americans to occupy Hungary when the war was over.

One nice clear quiet day, our relative peace was again disturbed by the sudden appearance of two German fighter planes flying very low, directly above us. For me, the aerial extravaganza of bombers or fighter planes right over our heads was the highlight of the war. To be a witness to such aerial thunder was a wonder. Most of the time, I was so fascinated by the fighting machinery itself I did not think about the fact that there were men inside those planes.

My mother commanded us to throw ourselves to the ground, but we soon realized they weren't shooting or bombing. Despite her insistence to stay down, I got up anyway and saw something I will never forget. Not far from my grandmother's land, just outside of town over the cornfields, a bi-wing Russian aircraft was flying very low and slow. The plane, a World War I relic, had an open cockpit with two pilots in it. Amazingly, the Germans did not shoot it down, most likely realizing the aircraft was no threat to them. Judging from the German 109's maneuvers, they were going to force the bi-wing into a cornfield and capture the pilots alive instead.

It didn't take them long before the Russian pilots were forced to land. By that time, several German Army vehicles full of soldiers made their way to the area and captured the Russian pilots. No one knew whether the Russians were on reconnaissance flight or just trying to go AWOL. The Germans stripped all the instruments immediately and left the abandoned plane in the cornfield.

My brother and I begged Mother to let us go to see the plane up close, but to no avail. We even made several attempts to sneak over there, but she caught us every time.

Ten days after the forced landing, the Germans took the plane apart and hauled it away in a truck.

By 1944, we could hear the heavy cannons firing in the distance and tried to guess whether they were Russian, Hungarian, or German by the slight variation in sound. The discussion shifted from if there was going to be war to how we were going to survive the actual fighting, explosions, and bombs of the armies all around us.

My parents feared the end of the world was coming for us no matter what the outcome.

Because my father was the head of the railroad greenhouse gardens, which employed 200 to 300 people, mostly women now that the bulk of the men were soldiers, he wasn't called in or drafted until Germany was losing the war on both the Eastern and Western fronts. When he was called to fight with the Germans, he was sent to the Russian front where they routinely sent Hungarians as well as other ethnic soldiers under German occupation to fight the Russians. As a result, thousands of Hungarian soldiers were killed by the Russians, having been sacrificed by the Germans who'd forced them front and center.

The rest of us—my mother, grandmother, grandfather, sister, brother, and I remained behind, awaiting what we feared was the inevitable.

LIFE DURING WARTIME

With my father gone to war, we decided it best to hunker down in what we called the Gatekeeper's House at the edge of Grandma's five acres. Built halfway into the ground and used to store supplies and as a guardhouse to deter people from stealing fruit from the orchard, it was accessed by several steps leading downwards and had a plant-eye view from windows set ten inches from the earth.

It was late 1944 when we set up permanent residence. I was attending Sámsoni Úti elementary school amidst the sounds of war—cannons, guns, hand grenades etc., that were ever present and growing closer and closer. German tanks and trucks passed through in all directions.

One fateful day, after nearly four years of sporadic bombing, the war reached us. Two hundred yards away from the Gatekeeper's House, a German tank was set up facing the Apafa forest to the north. We thought it strange because everyone expected the Russians to come from the east. Unbeknownst to us, a second tank had parked in front of the house we'd abandoned. We counted eight German soldiers preparing for something. What exactly, we couldn't be sure, until we realized the Russian army had reached the line of hills running north and south of us and had stopped behind it.

In my seven-year-old wisdom, I assumed it was because they were afraid.

Night came and all was quiet but for the occasional airplane, sporadic machine gun burst, and distant cannon fire. We had no idea how many soldiers were tucked away in the hills behind us. All we knew was we'd counted the eight Germans near our big house. We also knew we were situated directly between the Germans and the Russian armies.

"God save us!" my mother repeated, over and over again, hugging my brother and me to her body. She then shaved my twelve-year-old sister's head and dressed her in my father's clothes so she would look like a boy.

"Why are you doing that?" I asked.

"I'll explain later," she said.

I remember thinking it was odd and I'd never seen a girl with bald head before, but there was little time to give it much more thought.

My mother made a bed underneath the old iron stove for my brother and me. Even though we were practically below ground, Mother thought it safer there where the iron might protect us from stray bullets or who knew what else.

My brother was five years old and fell asleep easily on an old blanket she laid down for us. I couldn't comprehend the potential danger, much less what was to come. In my mind, the Germans were basically good. After all, they had given me chocolate. I also liked their gray and black uniforms. I was more than a little curious about what would happen. Besides, I'd never even seen a Russian before. In fact, I was so excited I couldn't sleep. In my mind, I couldn't wait to see the war. I was not only going to get to witness it as it happened, but from the very center of it all.

Truth be told, I couldn't believe my luck!

As we waited for the worst to happen, I crept over to the window and gazed into the darkness, as though waiting for the opening scene of a movie.

"Do you want to get killed?" my mother hissed, pulling me away. "They'll think you're an enemy soldier and shoot you dead."

Soldier? I thought. *Maybe that's what I'll be some day!*

As dawn approached, I heard a sound like I'd only ever heard in movies—a gruesome medieval cacophony of shouting, machine-gun fire, cannon burst, and pounding footfalls. Russians ran, en masse, over the hill in our direction.

There were no shouts from the German tanks and soldiers behind the big house.

Bullets began to strafe our Gatekeeper's House. Tile shattered as gunfire from the Russian side hit the roof. A large bullet came through the wall, was slowed by the plaster, and plinked ominously on the iron stove. Still hot, it dropped onto my sleeping brother's chest and the blanket covering him began to smoke.

Thank God, Istvan woke up unhurt.

Grandfather sat motionless on his bed in the bedroom until Grandma and Mother forced him to go under the bed for safety.

"Heads under the stove!" Mother commanded the rest of us.

Pieces of wall, roof, and debris rained down on us. I looked up and saw the daylight and dark gray clouds through where the ceiling had been blown away. We could see the Big House, 600 meters away, with a large gaping hole in it clear through the walls. Through the hole, I saw there was a second German tank parked right in front.

The eight German soldiers we'd counted the day before did their best to hold off what looked and sounded like a swarm of armed locusts coming across the hill. Suddenly, the tank that had been visible exploded and burned. The soldiers tried to escape. One managed to get away, while another dangled from the side of the tank. I watched him fall off as it maneuvered.

For him, the war was over.

With the Germans gone, the shooting stopped.

We were dusty, scared, and bruised, and starving. Miraculously, we were otherwise unhurt. Suddenly, we heard Russians yelling around our Gatekeeper's House. Six or seven burst through our door and soldiers poured in. They lined us up against the wall and pointed guns at us, even my little brother. We all thought we were done for as they ransacked what little we had. My mother and sister were crying. My grandmother screamed at the soldiers to put down their guns.

Needless to say, the soldiers ignored her. In fact, they helped themselves to anything and everything they fancied: food, clothes, and even a cheap little ring that was my sister's first ever piece of jewelry. Grandma tried to calm us by whispering not to worry and she had some hidden reserves for when things died down.

That was, until they stormed into the bedroom where Grandfather was hiding under the bed. A soldier stabbed the mattress with the bayonet at the end of his rifle. The bayonet did not go all the way through, but they found him cowering below.

Bald with round, gold-frame glasses, the Russians thought he was a German officer trying to hide. Especially after they began to interrogate him, and he answered in his confused jumble of different languages. At which point, they beat him savagely. We stood against the wall with several guns pointed at us, sure he was going to die, while we listened to the horrible screaming and hitting. My grandmother kicked fiercely and pulled on the soldiers, begging them not to hit him, saying he wasn't well, and indicating he was crazy.

The soldiers slammed the door closed and continued on.

Suddenly Grandpa went quiet.

As soon as the door swung open and the soldiers came out, Grandma rushed in.

She let out an anguished scream and began to cry.

I realized it was the first time I'd ever seen her cry.

Then, a Russian officer dressed in half-military, half-civilian clothing ordered the soldiers out, and to advance toward town. When they didn't go, he took his pistol and aimed it at the soldiers. As soon as they were gone, he surveyed the surroundings and assessed us. When he realized we were not a threat, he left as well.

We rushed into the bedroom to Grandpa, lying on the dirt floor in a pool of blood with half his skull shattered from the butt of a rifle. He was still alive, but barely.

My grandmother stabilized him as well as she could by wrapping his head in a bed sheet. He had lost a lot of blood and was in and out of a coma. He uttered words, but none that I could understand.

I couldn't possibly comprehend why my elderly, mentally challenged grandfather had been beaten all but to death by a mob of soldiers or why my grandma was left to take care of him as well as she could without any medical help or necessary supplies.

The anger and hostility I felt toward these barbarians was unimaginable, and there was still much more to come.

Another group of Russian soldiers entered the Gatekeeper's House and went straight to the window facing the Big House and the cornfield. Two other soldiers came to the window from the outside pulling a machine gun on two wheels. They placed the machine gun in the window and began shooting into the cornfield, the machine gun steaming up from the heat of the bullets.

When he ran out of bullets, the soldier quickly opened another boxful. He placed the end of the chain of bullets into the gun, then turned around and looked at me and my little brother. He picked up Istvan, placed him up in the windowsill between the machine gun and the new box of bullets, and ordered him to feed the gun by holding the chain of bullets coming out of the box. As a result, the gun cooled some and he was able to shoot two more boxes of bullets into the cornfield, totally mowing it down.

The whole time, my mother cried and screamed in fear for my brother's life. Had there been any Germans in the field shooting back, he would have been shot and killed.

When the soldier was done, he took off running. Another dragged the machine gun away. My mother ran to the window as quickly as she could and pulled my brother down to the safety of the floor.

When my mother wasn't looking, I scanned the open field, and watched the Russian army advance toward our Big House and the city beyond, some of them climbing on the abandoned German tank as they passed. There were endless armed hordes—thousands of men, trucks, tanks, and cannons headed toward Debrecen. They were also Hungarian peasant horse-drawn wagons full of non-military items they had taken from families like ours as they passed through. The soldiers looked more like marauding hoards than any kind of army. A lot of the Russians were not fully in army uniforms but wearing civilian clothes and boots. Some even wore German army coats removed from dead soldiers along the way. In addition to the clothes, food, furniture, and household goods, there were animals: chickens, geese, sheep, pigs, and larger animals like cows and horses tied to wagons. There were soldiers with guns hanging from their backs pushing bicycles so loaded down with goods, they could barely move them.

At one point, German cannons began firing from the nearby Apafa forest. In the ensuing chaos, the Russians abandoned everything in their possession except for the guns and hid behind anything wider than their own bodies.

The shelling from the Germans lasted only ten minutes.

The *glorious* Soviet Army didn't move for a long time, regrouping until they could calm the terrified horses, goats, cows, and assorted frenzied livestock.

Intermittently, Russians continued to bust into the Gatekeeper's House and frighten us by shouting and aiming guns at us in search of food we didn't have. We quickly put our hands up as soon as they came in. We adjusted out of necessity to the insanity of war. To me, it was more like chaos with half a roof and no food to eat—other than the secret stash my grandmother was keeping her eye on and willing to remain hidden.

It had been obvious to her from the start the Russians would win this battle because there were, "As many of them as the blades of grass in the fields," but she would not break into the promised stash until the Russians advanced toward Budapest, Vienna, and then Germany, leaving our little piece of Hungary.

By late afternoon on that never-ending day of chaos, Grandma decided she would go down to the Big House while it was daylight to see what damage had been done and to try and bring back some food, if any still existed. Since the Russians were also in and out of that house, we had no idea what she would find or see.

There were no civilians in sight, and we feared she would be shot, so we begged her not to go. Determined, she found a red scarf, took a broomstick, and attached the scarf to it.

"They wouldn't shoot at someone carrying a Russian flag, would they?" she bravely pronounced and lifted her broomstick high.

Before emerging from the Gatekeeper's House, she put the make-shift flag of the proletariat out the door, holding it high. As soon as she was convinced she could make it, she headed for the big house, looking like she was in the Russian Revolution of 1917 on her way to kill the Czar. Like a good revolutionary sacrificing for the good of the people—in this case the survival of her family and to avenge the near death of her husband—we watched Grandma progress down the narrow path, which divided the property into even halves. She turned the corner and disappeared behind the Big House.

Ten minutes passed.

Then half an hour.

Forty-five minutes went by.

I thought I saw her through the hole in the big house, but I couldn't be sure.

My mother and sister started to cry.

"She shouldn't have gone," my mother said, sobbing. "She's going to lose her life for us."

My brother brought a chair and we watched through the window, only seeing the stragglers who continued to march toward the city limits.

Nearly an hour passed before we spotted the red flag from around the corner of the big house. To this day, I will never forget the dark rainy clouds, the drizzle, or the ever-present sounds of war around us, but the sight of my heroic grandmother returning to us with a large sack on her shoulder looms largest, by far.

As she labored under the weight of multiple large bags on her shoulder, she still held the large red scarf with one hand. As we relieved her of the heavy load, the red scarf fell to the floor. She kicked it into the wet rubble where the roof had collapsed.

Grandma returned with some sugar and spices but no food. My brother and I jumped on the sugar, but we were yanked away from it by my mother who feared it had been poisoned by the Germans. She might have been right. The Germans and the Russians did horrible things like throw booby-trapped pens out of airplanes that kids picked up, only to have them explode in their hands.

We peppered Grandmother with questions: "What did you see? What did you find out?"

Distress etched her face. "There's a big cannon hole that went right through. Thick dust and broken bricks are everywhere. The furniture was shot up with machine guns. The dishes are all over the house, and most of the porcelain is broken, as though it was thrown against the walls."

"Grandma, what about the piano?" my sister Irén cried.

Our family piano was my sister's life. She played it every chance she had. My parents were very proud of her and always said she would grow up to be a concert pianist.

"Was it taken? Did they steal it?"

"No, my child," Grandma said. "I'm afraid it's worse."

My parents and grandma purchased the concert-quality grand piano a few years earlier, after Hitler took France and then Poland. War seemed inevitable and they knew they had to do something to ensure the family's future, so they invested in an incredible masterpiece of a piano.

Besides the four-bedroom house in Szerencs where my sister and I were born, the piano was their most prized possession. Long, black, and sleek, it had a lid with inlaid mother of pearl butterflies and flowers surrounded by a brass trim. We called it Franz Josef's piano because it was a work of art. They'd planned to hang onto it through the war and then sell it after to give us a fresh start, never expecting my sister would be such a talented player.

"Tell me," my sister begged.

Grandma coughed to keep herself from crying.

"They tore off the top lid and broke it to pieces," she managed before the tears broke through. "They defecated on the strings in three places and a lot of the others are shattered. Almost all the black keys are broken off."

My sister and mother wailed.

"It had to be the Russians," my grandma said. "The Germans would never do anything like that."

"What about the German tank on the other side of the house?" I asked.

"It's abandoned."

Despite it all, I couldn't help but want to climb all over it and even go inside of it. "What do you think happened to the soldiers?"

We ate whatever we could scrounge or mother and grandmother could concoct from practically nothing. I asked Grandma about her miracle food stash, but she was secretive about it. I was beginning to wonder if there really was food somewhere or if she was just trying to keep our hopes up. She knew armies always left occupational forces behind to keep their captured territories, so there were still a lot of soldiers securing the area and capturing Hungarian and German soldiers who were hiding out. She kept saying, "Not yet. There are still too many Russians around."

Midmorning one day, I heard screaming and cursing outside. We all rushed out and saw two Russian officers climbing on a ladder up to the attic of the Gatekeeper's House where part of the roof still existed. I remember both of them had on beautiful full-length leather coats that didn't look right on them, which meant they'd been removed by some unlucky dead German officers.

My grandmother screamed at the two Russians to get off the ladder, even climbing after one of them to try and pull him down. Then, one of them took out his pistol and shouted back at her in Russian. When he shot near her into the ground, she climbed down but kept on cussing at them. In the meantime, my mother huddled with us behind a tree so we wouldn't get shot and shouted at Grandma to stop her attack on the Russians.

That's when I realized my heroic grandmother was trying to protect our last bite of stored food. My stomach growled as I wondered what was up there and waited for the Russians to reappear. When they did, the first one pointed his gun at us. The other emerged holding a big, round Torontaly cheese. Golden and bigger than a wagon wheel, it was so heavy, the Russian could hardly carry it.

It could feed half the Russian army, I thought, as the Russians took off with our food, *but it will not feed us.*

SURVIVAL PLANS

We had no food, no heat, and had only a partial roof over our heads. Worse, Russian soldiers were everywhere. The desperation of uncertainty started to settle in my head. When and how was it going to end?

My grandmother and mother began to strategize. Mother figured most of the Russian Army were coming from the east and had already made it into the area. She assumed they were occupying Debrecen on their way through Hungary, and headed west through Austria, and then toward Germany to meet up with the Americans to defeat the Germans.

I think this was the first time I heard the word Americans. The word alone sounded reassuring, although it was unsettling to hear my mother and grandmother talking like military strategists. They figured if we headed east in the direction the Russians had come from, we would be safer than if we stayed put. Mother thought we should head about ten kilometers to the large Kovacs family farm, where they would surely help us out. Assuming they were still alive.

The plan had one major hurdle, however. "What are we going to do with Dad?" my mother kept asking. "He cannot walk, and we cannot carry him."

Grandpa was near death, and we couldn't leave him by himself, so we stayed in our decimated fortress for several days, just looking out the windows at the Russians swarm like locusts toward the city. Because the Germans had retreated from the onslaught—blowing up bridges, roads, factories, and destroying anything they considered valuable as they fled—there was no resistance. There was also no help from the Hungarian Army, who, thanks to the Germans, had been conscripted and sent to the Russian front.

After a few days, Grandma and Mother came up with a plan: Grandma and my sister Irén would stay with Grandpa while my mother, Istvan, and I would make the journey to the Kovacs's for help and, hopefully, find food we could bring back home.

"God help us," Mother kept saying, as the three of us emerged from our ground-level sanctuary, started up the stairs, and headed into the unknown for the first time since the Russian invasion.

We walked down the path for a half block, crossed the hot water ditch from the underground thermal springs near our home, and headed eastward. We saw several Russian soldiers bathing in the run-off from the thermal baths in town, but we didn't hesitate to continue past them.

Although the journey put us in great danger, I saw it as an adventure and couldn't help but be fascinated by the weaponry as it went by. We even saw a truck with two wheels up front that was tank chain driven from the back. The painted swastikas on the doors had been scratched off, but it had obviously been taken from the Germans. The weapons were a sight to behold, but not the soldiers who carried them. They had harmed my grandpa, which I would never forget and could never forgive.

As we made our way into the countryside, the Russians kept on coming, many with an abundance of spoils like clothes, bicycles, and even stacks of dishes taken from poor Hungarian families. It made our journey feel hopeless. Even if we were able to get some food from the Kovacs's, I figured these soldiers would just take it away from us.

We approached a forested area with trees on both sides of the road where the soldiers seemed to be camping in place instead of marching toward Debrecen. Just past a turn in the road, we came upon a group of Russians in an area littered with blown apart equipment, trucks, and a burned-out motorcycle with a side car. Soldiers were lined up awaiting their meals from a makeshift army kitchen fashioned from a large container with a built-in fireplace. It had wheels so it could be towed. As we went by, we saw a Russian soldier enjoying his food while sitting on a dead German soldier's chest. The German still had his helmet on his head.

My brother and I gaped in disbelief until Mother yanked on our arms. Without moving her lips, she warned us, "Keep moving. Keep your eyes on the road."

We reached the Kovacs's farm, which had remained intact. Mr. Kovacs told us the Russians had taken both of his horses, two of his fattened pigs, and a lot of his chickens and geese. I figured the soldiers we'd seen on the roadside were probably feasting on his livestock.

Thankfully, the family still had some supplies to share— bacon, kolbasz, flour, and some newly hatched baby geese. I put four of the little hatchlings in my big pockets and so did my brother. We packed everything they gave us tightly around our bodies and covered ourselves with big coats so we appeared to be carrying nothing.

Supremely thankful to the Kovacs family, Mother swore we would reciprocate their goodwill after the war.

The trip was harrowing and took all day, but it felt like we'd embarked on the road to hope and survival. When we returned to Grandmother, Irén, and Grandfather we were able to share a moment of genuine happiness and elation. As they took inventory of the food, rationing it so it would last as long as possible, my brother and I collected grass and greenery for our nine little baby geese, gave them water, and turned a little corner of the house into a nursery.

"The start of a flock," said Grandma.

HELLOS AND GOODBYES

As the sounds of war moved further toward the west, we began the process of cleaning the mess in the Gatekeeper's House. While the bulk of the Russian army headed toward Budapest and onto Austria, there were plenty of Russian soldiers left behind in Debrecen —enough to occupy the city, and to keep us on high alert.

Grandma made many trips down to the Big House. After a while, she deemed it safe for us to all go down, which we did with the utmost curiosity. I could hardly wait to look at the German tank in front of the big house just on the other side of the garden. I wasn't allowed to get near it under any circumstances, though.

We had to remain vigilant. Grandmother's land was fenced in, but not much of a deterrent for the Russian soldiers. They knew the hot water ditch flowed in front of our house and jumped the fence as they pleased instead of going around it to wash themselves. In fact, soaking and getting drunk while relaxing in the hot water became a favorite escape for the soldiers, particularly given its proximity to the large permanent base they'd begun to construct a half-kilometer from our property.

My grandmother was understandably concerned about the safety of my mother and sister. My brother and I did not understand why we were not included in that concern, until we started to overhear news of drunkenness and rape in the neighborhood by soldiers and at the surrounding farms. There were stories about soldiers inquiring about which farms had daughters of age or young wives and demanding wine and their daughters or wives at gunpoint.

Some of these incidents ended up in murder if the husband or father defended the female members of their family. While we were young kids and did not comprehend the reason why these things would happen, we knew it was smart to keep my mother and sister in the house as much as possible.

As things settled into a new, if tenuous, existence, Grandma somehow bartered her way into a very special purchase named Fancy. Fancy was a big, beautiful cow with red and white patches, big black eyes, long eyelashes, an intelligent face, and a white curlicue which fell down her forehead. Fancy the cow would go on to singlehandedly sustain us through the dark years, those terrible years, of Russian occupation with fresh warm milk, cream, butter, sour cream, and cheese curd.

When she came to us, we concocted a covered place for her which couldn't quite be called a barn. It did not have walls but was more like a covered parking space. Fancy gave us all the creations Mother and Grandma could create from her oversized milk factory. In return, we did everything we could to make her comfortable. She loved to be pampered and have her hide scratched. When she saw the scraper made of steel with a row of small teeth, she would stretch her neck straight out.

Grandma would milk Fancy at the crack of dawn. My brother and I oversaw feeding and watering her, as well as cleaning her stall. We always fought over who would do the dirty work. I tried to talk Istvan into agreeing I should do the front chores for Fancy, and he should do the back one. Needless to say, he would not go for that except on the occasions when I was able to bribe him with something he wanted.

I loved Fancy and liked to take her grazing. Because Grandma's land did not have a grassy area, I had to take Fancy to the roadside in front of the house so she could graze on the banks of the ditches. Grandma instructed me to tie her front feet loosely together like a hobble so she couldn't go on other people's land and eat their crops. I preferred to tie her two horns with a long rope and tell her she could not go into the cornfield—a gentle pull on her tether always worked. I could talk to her, and I knew she understood me.

Fancy was as smart as my Rio, our German shepherd and Komondor mix pup. If I took the two of them out to the roadside for Fancy to graze, both stayed right by me. The dog would sound a warning bark when a Russian army vehicle went by. Rio knew not to like or trust them either. I was sure Rio would tear them to pieces if they tried to take our cow, but I still worried every time a truck approached us on the road.

I felt lucky to have both creatures and considered them friends.

We were busy working on the Big House cleanup one spring day in 1946. It was a huge undertaking we did bits at a time. I remember being in the big bedroom. We called it that because my parents slept there, but it really wasn't any bigger than ours. The tall window was broken, frame and everything. As I looked through the blown-out panes, I spotted an emaciated man with a long beard and assumed he was a homeless person seeking food or shelter.

At first, I was afraid.

And then Mother recognized him.

The next thing I knew, I had jumped into his arms.

Father was alive!

He'd returned to us all in one piece!

We learned he'd been captured by the Russians along with another officer, but they managed to escape what he'd later describe as a barbaric hell.

I was no longer afraid of anything, not even the Russians. Father was back!

With Father home, I could now investigate the tank sitting just meters in front of the house. I had been sneaking glances at it whenever my mother wasn't watching. I'd daydreamed about making it my personal property but hadn't been allowed near it. Lucky for me, my father was just as curious as I was.

He climbed up onto it first, taking very careful steps as he went around the top and over the cannon. He peered into the open cover where the soldiers got in.

"You can't be too careful. It could be booby trapped," Father said taking his time to observe the interior. "The soldiers who abandoned it want to kill any enemy soldiers who might try to confiscate it."

When he dangled his feet inside, my breathing almost stopped. My heart pounded like a drum as he carefully lowered himself into the tank.

The minutes felt like hours until I heard him say, "It looks alright."

I let out a huge sigh of relief. "Can I climb up?"

"Not yet," echoed from inside.

Another minute went by. Then two. I glanced back at the house and saw my grandmother, sister, and mother watching through one of the closed windows. I could practically hear my mother say, "What is he doing, risking his life and that of his own child?"

Suddenly, a wooden case emerged from the top door lid of the tank. It was full of bottles. My father climbed out of the tank, case in hand, with a huge smile on his face.

"Champagne!" he announced.

I could hear a sigh of relief from the house.

"We'll have a party!" yelled mother, as he took the case down and put it on the ground.

"We cannot drink this stuff," Father said. "It might be poisoned."

He proceeded to break the necks off the bottles and pour good, French champagne into the grass. There was no risking more danger than we'd already faced.

"Now can I go up, Dad?" I asked.

"You may," he said. "Be careful, though. It's all steel in there, so don't hurt your head and don't move anything—no switches or levers. Not one."

Despite my nerves, I felt enormously brave as I dropped down into the seemingly indestructible steel beast. As large as it was from the outside, there was little interior space, and it was difficult to move around. I was incredibly tempted to touch the instruments and try the levers, but I appreciated my father's trust in me. I simply sat in awe, wondering what had happened to the soldiers who had left it behind. Surely they had been punished severely. That is, if they were still alive.

"Come on out," I finally heard my father call. "We have work to do."

As I looked around from the tank's tower opening, I felt all powerful. For a moment, I decided when I grew up, I was going to be a tank driver. But also a fighter pilot.

I climbed out, walked around on top, and touched the cannon and some of the machine guns protruding from the tank's body. I thought about how these soldiers must have felt trying to hold back thousands of Russians. Did they know my family was in the middle of the crossfire? In my mind, I was sure they would be pleased to know we were still alive.

When I jumped off the tank to the ground, I saw my father examining the large, thick, one square meter steel panels which hung off the body of the tank to protect the wheels and chain of the running gear.

He began to remove them.

"What are we going to use those for?" I asked.

"Let's get them off and I'll explain when the time is right."

There were a lot of panels, and it took us all day to remove them. We put them into a wheelbarrow and stacked them up behind the shed, one by one, so they could not be seen from the street. When we finished, it was almost dark.

"Let's go take a look at the other tank," he said, and we headed for the other abandoned German behemoth in the cornfield not very far from our house.

The tank had suffered interior damage, but it also had those protective steel panels around the sides.

"We'll leave this one for tomorrow."

The next day we were out early liberating that tank from its protective shields as well. My father did not climb inside and did not let me, either. He worked fast, not wanting anyone to see us doing this, especially any of the Russian soldiers from the nearby base.

When we finished, there were three big stacks of panels behind the shed. We covered them with hay and straw so they looked like a haystack—nothing that would attract curious eyes.

My father began to plug the gaping hole that went through the house. Material, like bricks and wood, came from houses and buildings that had been demolished from the fighting. My brother Istvan and I were given hammers and other tools to clean the bricks. Father brought in clay from the hot water ditch. When the wall was done, the windows were fixed, and the house was totally cleaned of debris and dust. The piano was also cleaned, but the top with the mother of pearl decoration could never be fully repaired.

During this time, my father nearly lost his life to a Russian soldier who showed up drunk and insistent he be supplied with "wine and women." My father knew better than to just walk away or tell him to go away or fight with him. Instead, he stood as close as possible so the Russian couldn't lift the rifle and shoot him. While he tried to placate the brute, he continued to stand as close as possible to the old rifle so it would have gone through his armpit. Finally, some higher-ranking sober Russians came by and ordered the man to go away.

With the incredible willpower, tenaciousness, and bravery of my parents and grandmother, the rehabilitation of our lives was well underway. Unfortunately, Grandpa Ferenc whose first name became my middle name when I was christened, passed away at Christmas time that year. It had been several months since he'd sustained a broken skull inflicted by the Russian soldiers, but his wounds never healed and he never recovered.

WAR BABIES

My little baby sister Zita was conceived like so many others during the uncertainty that was the aftermath of World War II. She was named for my mother's favorite Hungarian film and stage actress Szeletski Zita (whom she actually got to meet in person when she came to visit me in the United States many years later).

We had our own war baby and many more of the animal variety being born and hatched all the time. Our geese, once downy and yellow-haired, grew white feathers practically before our eyes. And then we had chickens, not just one to slaughter and eat, but several young ones who could then multiply. Out of this first batch of chickens King Steven was born. King Steven grew up very quickly to rule his flock. He was a beautiful large red rooster with gorgeous black tail feathers.

Trespassing Russian visitors couldn't see our livestock. Unfortunately, they could hear their playful honks. The older our geese got, the more noise they made, which attracted the members of the People's Army, who by this time, were already being referred to as the Liberators of the Hungarian People and the glorious Soviet Red Army—or so the constant propaganda on radio and in newspapers—informed us.

Because these barbarians crisscrossed our private domain at will, it wasn't long until we were awakened from our sleep by the sound of agitated geese. We ran out to see what was causing the disturbance and were confronted by armed Russian soldiers. Two soldiers held us at gunpoint while a third soldier caught each goose, took the captured bird by the head, and whirled it around by the neck until it was lifeless. The last guy cut its head off with a sword and then threw it down so the blood would trickle out on to the ground.

We watched helplessly as they killed all our geese and hauled them away toward their base in three large potato sacks dripping with blood.

Our whole family gathered any kind of old wood and mesh wire we could find. We even took some wood planks from our fence. We collected the materials from bombed outhouses with no owners around. We had to survive so taking a few pieces of wood from a totally destroyed building was not a consideration— survival was. I liked to believe the owners had escaped before the Russians came and were living well in some remote village, farm, or in the mountains.

Out of these materials, my father began to create cubicles with wire doors which he lined up next to each other near the well.

"What are we going to put into them?" I asked my father as I handed him a piece of wood, nail, or a hammer.

"Rabbits," he said.

"Rabbits?"

"Your mother wants us to raise Angora rabbits—you know, the ones that grow long, fine, white hair. To eat, but mostly so your mother can cut the hair off the rabbits every so often and make yarn out of their fur. She, your sister, and your grandmother will knit sweaters. We 'll keep some and sell some."

"How do you make yarn?" I asked.

"The way people have made yarn for hundreds of years using lamb's wool, silkworm thread, and several other natural materials."

In other words, I would see once we had the rabbits!

The first row of cages was covered with chicken wire and all had a door. To create two more rows of five cages, we children were told to keep our eyes out for nails, no matter how rusty or bent. It took weeks, but we scrounged up the necessary materials and Father was able to build fifteen rabbit cages.

Three days later, Mother came home with a basket full of cute little white rabbits.

My brother and I were tasked with caring for them by following Mother's careful instructions. "Give them a lot of grass and they should have lots of water too. And keep their cages clean, they mustn't be dirty!"

The rabbits grew fast. Pretty soon a wooden yarn-making machine appeared in the house. It worked by pushing a foot pedal, like the old Singer sewing machine that had been my mother's wedding present in 1932.

It took a while, but soon the ladies in the family produced a large basket of yarn. Then, they all started to knit. Even Irén, the self-appointed queen of the family, learned how and pitched in!

Unfortunately, our happy rabbit enterprise was short lived. One of our constant trespassers must have seen our lovely white

Angora rabbits because, one morning, as we approached the cages to feed the rabbits, Father sent us directly back to the house.

Russians had begun to remove the rabbits from their cages and hit them over the head with a big stick.

I snuck around the corner just as my father was trying to talk them into stopping. I watched as one of the Russians turned his machine gun toward my father and let out a blast of bullets inches from his feet into the ground.

The soldiers killed all but five of our precious rabbits. After all, the most popular slogan for Communism, fostered by the Russians was, "Everything belongs to the people."

Apparently, *they* were the people.

We were not.

As they were leaving, the soldier with the machine gun shot another round into the air in my father's direction.

One day, a Hungarian peasant driving a one-horse wagon entered Grandma's yard. The wagon was covered with planks with some hay on top. It backed up to the old pig house where we'd housed pigs before the war. The man took the cover off the wagon, opened the back, and revealed the longest pig I ever saw. She had very short blond hair. She was also very pregnant.

We instantly started to call her Piggy.

Piggy was coaxed off the wagon and all of us guided her into her new home, Piggy Palace. We put down hay for her to lie on, filled a trough with water, and gave her some dry corn on the cob, which she devoured instantly.

"It would be nice if she would have about twelve piglets," Mother said. "We will keep some and trade off the rest. Then, we'll be able to get glass and other materials for something your father wants to build."

We pampered Piggy with every bit of food we could give her and could hardly wait for her piglets to arrive. Piggy really liked Piggy Palace. A few times we wanted to let her out, but she didn't even want to leave. She was completely content.

One morning at dawn, we were awakened by Rio, the dog, making an incredible racket. We all ran out and saw the reason for the noise—a soldier was standing at Piggy Palace surveying our precious Piggy. Mother tried to send us back to the house, but we didn't move. Tired of losing our pets and livestock, we were going to defend Piggy with every ounce of strength we had, and made enough noise to chase away the Russians.

About eleven the next morning, however, four soldiers showed up on a horse-drawn wagon, which they backed up to Piggy Palace. Our screaming and cussing were of no avail. They yelled back at us in Russian and pointed their guns at us. My sister started to cry. My brother and I looked for rocks, anything to throw at the thieves, but mother stopped us from attacking them. The Grand Red Army, who was supposed to free us from the German occupation, stole our Piggy.

Then, a miracle happened! About mid-afternoon that same day we heard Rio barking, not in anger but in a happy playful manner around Piggy Palace. I rushed there to see what was happening. Lo and behold, there was Piggy in her triumphant glory, waiting for someone to open the door for her. She had escaped her captors and come home!

We fed her, scratched her back, and washed her, which she loved. The word got out to some nearby neighbors about what had happened, and they came to see if it was really true.

Our happiness lasted for three days, until the four Russians showed up again with their wagon. This time, Piggy put up a real fight. It took the soldiers half an hour to get her on the wagon. Piggy fought hard and she bit one of them. We were happy about that but miserable watching Piggy cry her heart out, her legs tied this time.

Piggy created an encore that afternoon, appearing once again at the entrance to Piggy Palace. Rio was ecstatic and wanted to play with her, but our beloved escape artist and hero did not want to participate. Even though we were glad to see her back, we were sad. We knew this was not the end. My grandma even went to some of the neighbors to see if one of them would take Piggy and hide her. None of the neighbors wanted to cooperate, fearing retribution by the soldiers. Like us, most of them had already gone through similar ordeals with their animals.

Knowing she only had a few hours of freedom, we gave her all the food and water she wanted, scratched her back, and bathed her. She was happy, but we were sad. To us, it was like the last supper. We knew she would not live long enough to bring her babies to life.

The soldiers showed up again and we never saw Piggy again.

Not too long after losing our beloved Piggy, I realized there was activity at the abandoned tank in the field, furthest from our house. This time, a group of female Russian soldiers busied themselves around the German tank.

My brother and I wanted to investigate but weren't allowed to go figure out what they were doing. I decided they were going to tow the tank away, but after about three hours of activity, an old truck appeared, gathered up all the soldiers, and drove a distance away. Ten minutes later, there was a large explosion—larger than I ever remembered hearing at the height of the war. When the dust and debris settled, the German tank had been blown into pieces.

The next morning, I awoke to shouting in Russian. I spotted the female soldiers again and thought, *Oh, God they're going to blow up the other tank sitting right in front of the big house.* Thankfully, when the same old rusty Russian military truck reappeared, they left two of the lady soldiers with the tank.

At noontime, we heard a great ruckus. I rushed outside and saw they were attaching chains and cables to the tank. Then, a Russian tank pulled up in front of the German tank, and they attached them to each other. The Russian tank revved up, emitted a great deal of black exhaust smoke, and attempted to tow the bigger German tank. After several tries, they were able to tow it to the same site where the other tank had been destroyed and proceeded to blow it up, too.

The remains of the two German tanks were there for several weeks until two trucks appeared with over a dozen soldiers. Russian trucks followed them to the site in that open field. They picked up all the steel debris and hauled it away.

Somehow, I felt like the secret history of the German soldiers who were savvy and brave enough to hold back the thousands of Russians, if only for a night, had been destroyed as well. Were they really Nazis or just regular men brainwashed by a madman? I'd also imagined my father repurposing the steel behemoth into a giant till with the power of twelve horse-drawn plows, so I was sad to see it destroyed like that.

Worst of all, I could no longer boast at school about the German steel giants, which rested right outside my door.

THE GREENHOUSE

Grandma had nearly five acres of land capable of growing food. The future of our economy was unpredictable; it was unknown whether we would return to a state where people could work, make a living, and not starve to death. Growing our own food was imperative.

My mother, like my father, always worked. She cooked, cleaned, and made our clothes on her Singer sewing machine. She would take the clothes Irén had outgrown and if the color and material were adaptable for a boy, namely me, she would create something out of it. Nothing was ever wasted. When I grew out of something, my brother would get a new garment. As busy as she was, she always found time to foot race with us at sundown in the summers.

My parents were determined to not only restart our life but make it into the existence we enjoyed before the war. Because my father was a jack of all trades, my brother and I learned a lot of practical skills from working alongside him. We also learned nothing was impossible. His determination was infectious.

The ditch that carried excess hot groundwater from the city's public pools to the river was 600 feet away from our house. My father had a plan to use this valuable resource to our advantage by designing a year-round garden within three greenhouses that would be heated by the hot water going to waste right in front of our property.

One greenhouse would be placed perpendicular to the road behind the house. His plan would tap the hot water, so it flowed through all three greenhouses and then back out to the ditch. The other two greenhouses would be set up perpendicular to the first one in a U shape that would surround our house on all three sides.

Because the hot water was excess and had been diverted away to cool off as it made its way to the Kondoros creek several kilometers from our house, we weren't utilizing resources in a bad or illegal way. While still hot, the water would be run through all three of the greenhouses and back out to the ditch, keeping the greenhouses warm enough to grow things in them all year round.

At the time I did not realize what a tremendous undertaking this was going to be, and I had plenty of questions.

"How is the hot water going to flow in the greenhouses when it is higher than the ditch?" I asked.

"We will use the force of gravity, by digging out the dirt to make the main part of the greenhouses low like the Gatekeeper's House, so the hot water can easily flow in and through."

"Where are we going to put all the dirt we dig out?"

"I've already started to build a two-wheeled wagon that can carry a cubic meter of dirt at a time. We will fill up some lower areas out in the field near the Gatekeeper's House. I already managed to buy the two wagon wheels it needs. The rest I can make here if you help me."

"But we don't have a horse to pull the wagon."

"We don't need a horse. We are going to use Fancy. I am going to build a yoke for her. Everything is possible."

"Yes," I repeated, in awe of my father. "Everything is possible."

"We will need a lot of glass and some more used brick. With all the bombed-out houses, that shouldn't be too hard. We will also need wood, cement, and doors—some of which I can make myself."

"We have the flat pieces of metal we took off the tanks. Are we going to use them?" I asked.

"They are an important part of all this," he said with a huge smile that said I'd finally figured out a main feature of his master plan. "We are going to cover the canal that brings in the hot water from the ditch so there won't be steam, which isn't good for the plants."

To make sure I understood exactly what he was describing, I decided to go down to the Gatekeeper's House to see how it had been built into the ground. Istvan joined me. As we approached, we could see the roof that had been blown off the house was now repaired. My father, with the assistance of a neighbor, had fixed that too.

As we approached the Gatekeeper's House, we heard voices and laughter coming through the open windows. We were startled and thought perhaps some people had moved in without my family realizing it.

The noise and laughter grew louder as we grew closer. We also spotted steam coming through the window—the very same window where the soldiers had put my brother up to hold and feed the bullets into the machine gun.

We were scared and didn't know what to expect. We definitely did not want to be detected by the strangers there, but curiosity and our sense of adventure prevailed. We approached the house from an angle, thinking whoever was in there wouldn't be able to see us. We got to the corner of the house, laid down on the ground, and slowly crawled toward the open window, the bottom of, which was about a foot off the ground. My brother and I lifted our heads up slowly and peered inside.

To say we were startled, would be a serious understatement. There were eight or nine stark naked women bathing in hot water! In fact, their uniforms and guns had been hung up on the wall. In our Gatekeeper's House! Laughing and drinking and singing! Wearing nothing at all!

The same female soldiers who'd blown up the German tanks had the same idea as our father. They built a canal from the hot water ditch leading right into the Gatekeeper's House, which was lower than the hot water ditch itself. They'd flooded the Gatekeeper's House with the help of gravitation and repurposed the structure into a bathhouse!

To us, their ingenuity wasn't as much of a surprise as their anatomy. We'd never seen a naked woman before, not to mention a bunch of them! We definitely wanted to see more and did not hide ourselves as well as we should have.

"Hey!" one of them said, spotting us.

Their laughter turned into screaming and yelling in Russian. A couple of them stood up to chase us away.

For two young boys, agape at the sight of female anatomy, we couldn't believe they didn't try to cover themselves. In fact, we were so surprised, we simply froze, staring until one of them threw water at us through the open window. Even then, we didn't run. Finally, a large, robust lady in uniform came around the house, yelling and laughing at us in a threatening fashion.

"Where were you boys for so long?" Mother asked sternly when we returned home.

"We . . . we went down to the Gatekeeper's House to see how it was built . . . structurally," I stuttered. ". . . because we are going to help father build the new greenhouses the same way."

"Okay," she said, "But I told you two, do not go anywhere without telling me and don't pick up anything from the ground that looks like a bullet or a gun."

"We won't, Mother," we said in unison, never letting her or our father know we'd gone on a mission to learn about architecture and got an entirely different education.

I think of it as the one true benefit I got out of the war!

Father, Istvan, and I began to dig holes for the greenhouses. We dug until their bottoms were below the ditch. We then built a channel out of concrete and brick we collected from bombed out nearby structures. We covered these channels with the quarter inch steel panels from the destroyed tanks. Each of the panels were identical and about a square meter in size. Father designed the width of the channels so the panels would completely cover them, preventing the hot water from emitting steam into the greenhouse. The water heated the panels, which would create heat in the greenhouses vital for plant growth in the fall and winter.

When the greenhouses were done, we let the hot water in from the ditch and it flowed perfectly.

My parents and grandma were elated. My brother, father and I were heroes!

My father began to grow various plants in the greenhouses and outdoors on Grandma's lands. He also seeded almost an acre of alfalfa that became Fancy's winter food after it was dried by the sun.

In addition, Father planted carnations, violets, roses, and other flowers, which my grandmother and mother sold in the local farmer's markets and in front of cemeteries. Lucky for us there was a strong tradition of buying flowers to remember loved ones in Hungary, and we did a brisk business.

We often got up at five in the morning to pick flowers still covered in dew. Then, we would load up Grandmother's bicycle truck so she could push it to the market, sell our produce and flowers, and bring home the cash.

Mother worked in the garden and greenhouses with the flowers and the vegetables we grew for our own use. The vegetables were saved in the earthen bunker Father built during the war. When I think of all of it now, the land had saved us from the bullets of war and starvation. We had space to run and play with animals, pull up fresh vegetables like, kohlrabi, green onions, carrots and eat them raw. We even had enough to feed to Fancy the wonderful cow.

Many others weren't so lucky, especially anyone who lived in the city.

MODERN SLAVERY

Hungarians were full of hope once the war ended. People started to come alive with the possibility the Russians would go home, and we would rebuild the country.

School started up again. My mother enrolled me in a small elementary school not far from our house. I'd learned my ABCs at Csapo Kert, the old larger school, before the German army took over the building. Here, the teacher had the same large printed white poster where the capital and the small letters and numbers were printed in perfect black letters. I did not understand how printing was done so I wondered how someone could write such perfectly nice letters and I could not.

My school was located just off the highway from the new Russian army base. There was constant noise from construction and military vehicles heading back and forth to different parts of the city. We were warned to stay away from the road and not get close to the Russian soldiers or the vehicles.

"They're Communists," my parents would say about them and an increasing number of other people. "Don't go near them. They're bad."

It was hard not to be curious, at least about the soldiers, considering the old trucks always seem to break down near the school. Some of the Russian-made vehicles were from World War I and built in the '20s or early '30s. We also saw Dodge trucks that had come from the Americans, and never broke down.

The United States had equipped the Russians well against the Germans. Of course, the Russians were already motivated by a strong desire to defend their homeland and pay back the Germans for their longstanding brutality. Most people thought that without the Americans' help, the Germans would have defeated the Russians on their own turf, perhaps at the famous battle of Stalingrad.

It had to happen this way, people would say. The German and Hungarian Armies lost the war when the Russians came from the east and the Allied forces came from the west. The two stronger armies destroyed Hitler's schizophrenic ambitions and caused the German Army to collapse.

One thing we all knew for sure was the Russians would betray their friendly American allies, which is exactly what they did soon after the defeat of Germany. The Russians did not keep the Allied agreement that all occupying forces would go back to their own countries by 1947. Stalin, like Hitler, planned to eventually conquer Europe. As a result, American forces stayed in Europe, defending it from Russia until 1990 when the Soviet Union finally collapsed. Stalin, like Hitler, would not accomplish his goal of European domination, but the so-called Eastern-bloc countries were doomed to suffer under Russian Communist rule for decades.

More than eleven Hungarian political parties formed, one of which was the Hungarian Communist party, which had been started by the group who attempted a revolution against the Horthy regime (with the support of the Russians) in 1919. When they were defeated, they ran to Russia for refuge and were absorbed by the Russian Communist Party. Having overrun Hungary in the war, they were protected and sponsored by Stalin to return, emboldened in their mission.

Not long after I started back at school, the Hungarian National Railroad decided to reopen five of the large railroad garden divisions in the country. They'd started to clean up from the ravages of war, rebuilding the garden—including the buildings and greenhouses that had been demolished by bombs. The railroad wagon factory, where they built railroad cars, had also been demolished by the allied bombers along with the railroad station.

They wanted my father to take his old position back and run the railroad garden in Debrecen. Father was delighted to return to work until he learned that to get his rank back, he would have to join the Communist Party. They argued he could not be the leader of 200 or more people if he didn't become a Communist.

He refused.

My father was an ardent supporter of a very popular political organization called the Small Farmer's Party. He used his artistic talents to design placards for them and got involved personally. Their platform not only supported small farmers but had a forward-thinking philosophy that heavily supported and promised to work for entrepreneurship and industry. My father believed this party was the true salvation for the country.

At that time, a leader or manager of a government or people-owned company had to be a Communist party member, but he would not join. They threatened to put him in a low-level railroad job if he didn't join the Communist party. He refused. My father was demoted, but he accepted the menial job just to show them he wanted to be a dogma-free individual. Instead of my father who held a diploma in horticulture, they placed an uneducated, alcoholic party member who could be barely read or write in his position to manage the railroad gardens and its 250 workers. This type of incident was common; it happened across the whole country in all industries and environments.

Two or three agitators from the Communist party—which, by this time, was not really a party but the government of Hungary itself—would come to our house, sometimes multiple times a week, trying to entice him by offering his high-ranking job and full salary back. They would come late at night when they thought my brother, sisters, and I were asleep. We were in bed, but there was no sleeping as these men tried to coerce my father to become a Communist.

This went on for a year or more, but my father stood his ground. We kids learned a lot about what Communism truly was— a dictatorship full of empty promises. To me, *apparatchik* was another word for a low-rank gangster. And *Utopia*, it definitely wasn't.

Because they needed my father's expertise and knowledge of horticulture, they depended on him to run everything, but with an average laborer salary and without his rank. They continued to promise him his full salary and the return of his rank as soon as he became a member of the Communist party.

He never wavered.

The upside was since my father was, once again, a railroad man, our whole family was entitled to free rail travel. My father worked eight hours a day with the railroad, and was an amateur beekeeper, but it was the greenhouse that really kept us going. When winter approached, we used our ability to travel for free to supply green lettuce throughout the country. The whole family would pack our suitcases with lettuce and travel to Budapest. Resellers would line up at the train station waiting for us and our lettuce to take to their towns throughout Hungary.

After two years of Soviet occupation, it had become clear the Russians weren't going anywhere. The people of Debrecen and soon, Hungary in general, started to accept the unfortunate reality of the Russian occupation. It was obvious the Hungarian Communist Party was gaining the upper hand in every regard. Because they were backed by the Russians, the leaders were gaining considerable power. Some of the smaller parties fell away, particularly after the Communist party accused their leaders of crimes and started fictitious trials against them. A lot of opposing politicians were jailed or even executed for crimes they did not commit. Slowly, everything seemed to succumb or melt into the Communist Party. This was all done by the Russian dictatorship who directed the Hungarian Communist Party, which essentially governed the country.

My father's beloved Small Farmer's Party met the same fate as all the other groups. Their leaders were prosecuted, accused of treason, and declared to be the enemies of the people. Anyone who had anything to do with the former government or was a high-ranking officer in the former army or police had an uncertain future and had to be careful of everything he said or did.

Those who wanted to get ahead in the regime joined the Communist party. Some did it for survival, others for power, influence, connection, and cronyism to get ahead. In 1947, the Communist party leader Rákosi became the absolute ruler. Rákosi had been part of the 1919 Communist-led uprising, which was put down quickly, escaped to Russia, and marched back into Hungary in 1945 with the Soviet Army who made him president.

The Communists confiscated or nationalized factories, large homes, cars, big farms, and put heavy taxes on small businesses and farmers. Everything belonged "to the people." In the meantime, actual people were either broke because they couldn't pay the taxes and went to jail for it, or they submitted to the government, gave up their small business, and were maybe allowed to work there as an employee for a small salary.

Small farmers were forced to join government farm associations or TSZs, which meant their land was confiscated. Now they had to work their own land along with others for the "good of the people." Most of the crops and their value had to be given to the government. The large farms were simply given to the government with no compensation to their original owners. Those who didn't submit simply had their land taken away from them, and had to go to work on the collective farms for almost no money.

If an enterprising individual legitimately made money, or sold goods on the black market, he had to live with the possibility someone would turn him in. Such was the duty of a good Communist.

Wherever you worked, you had to fill out forms in which you had to give all kinds of information about yourself: your occupation, the political status of your father and mother before and after the war, etc. This was made a part of your record kept by the local Communist party; the record followed you no matter where you went to live or work.

Communism's hold in Hungary continued to grow. Hungary was an official puppet of the Soviets and, of course, Stalin. The Russian Army made sure Stalin's orders were carried out. Hungary became the Soviet Army and Air Force bastion. Because the Russians had already planned to stay in all the occupied countries and suck them dry of any wealth, Hungary became a virtual slave to the Soviets. The Russians burdened the Hungarian people and country by ordering them to pay restitution for "liberating" them from the Germans.

The Hungarian Communist government became the overseers of the Hungarian modern slave population. They controlled every facet of life. They put uneducated laborers and peasants in leadership or management positions in manufacturing or business. Former professionals were now considered non-persons—if they were lucky. Intellectuals and people who had success in the society before the war or were well to do were ridiculed, sometimes publicly. Their wealth was, of course, confiscated. Ex-high-ranking, educated citizens were picking cabbage for free in concentration camps while guards aimed machine guns at them. The intellectual segment of the nation was virtually eliminated. Uneducated people—workers and peasants— were in charge of politics as well as the economy.

Rákosi, bloodthirsty himself, but taking orders from Stalin, established the Hungarian Secret Police. They became known as the dreaded AVH or Állam Védelmi Hatóság, the so-called Government Defense Authority. In truth, they were just like the German SS in Nazi Germany. After all, Stalin had copied the Gestapo from Hitler, and called it the KGB.

People were disappearing for no reason, never to be seen again. Mock trials were created and broadcast on radio to scare even more people to line up and do as they were told. Torturing people to admit to false, mostly political, crimes was the order in the late forties and early fifties. People, neighbors, and workers were encouraged to turn in their friends and co-workers. False accusations were used to gain favors from the Communist party or to protect jobs. Sometimes children were forced to turn in their own parents.

Stalin had copied Hitler's approach exactly: The dogma, lies, and forced promises of propaganda were all around us. Portraits of Lenin, Stalin, and Rákosi seemed to be everywhere we turned. So was constant hammering of the praises of the great leaders, in the case of Hungary, that included the glorious, heroic Red Army's liberation of our country from Nazi occupation.

Unfortunately, the only way to get ahead in an environment like this was, as the old adage says, *if you can't beat 'em, join 'em.*

My father would do nothing of the sort.

Nor, as it turned out, would I.

THE BRAVES

Naturally, schools and education were completely under government control. The Communists put great emphasis on Soviet heroes, scientists, writers, etc. We were to learn little or nothing about Goethe, Edison, Washington, Einstein, or Shakespeare but heard all about and saw pictures of Marx, Engels, Lenin, Stalin, Rákosi, Pushkin, Michurin, Gorky, and others. These pictures hung in classrooms, city buildings, and street cars. Streets and cities were renamed after them. Enormous statues were erected of these leaders holding the Russian flag or waving the hammer and sickle. They were praised as gods. Every method of persuasion was used to pound dogma and Communist trash into children's heads.

The brainwashing started right from kindergarten—complete with the spiffy Pioneer uniforms made up of white military shirts, blue hats, short pants, and of course, the red triangle neckties. The Pioneers were organized similar to the Russian Pioneers and wore the same uniform as in the Soviet Union and the other satellites. The goal was the same too: build future Communists.

There were regular and frequent Pioneer meetings at Sámsoni Úti elementary where I went to second and third grade and at Fuvészkherty Átalànos iskola where I went to fourth, fifth, and sixth grade. There were parades on every Communist holiday, and we were obliged to participate. At school, we were taught Communist songs we had to sing and slogans we had to yell, whether we wanted to or not.

When Rákosi, came to Debrecen to make a speech, a podium was built in the center of town. The distance from the railroad station to the podium was about two kilometers. Along the route were two to three story buildings on both sides. In advance of his visit, the entire distance was draped from sidewalk level to the roof line with red cloth decorated with the hammer and sickle, and slogans like "Long Live the Glorious Soviet Union" and "World Proletariat Unite."

I grew into my early teen years doing what the other kids did: learning and obeying my teachers. At home it was a different story. I began to sense my parents were very dissatisfied with what was going on around us and how it affected their place in society. I began to pay more and more attention to the difference between what I absorbed in real life versus what I was told in school.

My parents often talked about the four-bedroom house they'd built in Szerencs. Talk of Szerencs always put a smile on my face because of my early memories of carefree play and the wonderful friends I had there and saw when we went back for visits. My grandfather and Aunt Juliska still lived there in the house.

I looked forward to our next trip knowing Aunt Juliska would make her special split pea soup with dumplings and parsley she picked from the garden. I always tried to help her pick peas, but she would tell me I didn't know which ones to pick. When her apron felt full enough, we went into the house where she would open each green pea pod and push the peas with her thumb into a dish filled with water. She allowed me to help her until I'd whisked one too many tender, soft, sweet peas into my mouth.

"Go out and spin wheels with your friends or something," she would say. "You've eaten so many peas, I'm going to have to go out and pick more to have enough to cook."

Reluctantly, I would go outside and play with my friends on the street in front of the house, never too far from one of the windows. I wanted to stay within hearing distance when Aunt Julia or Grandpa would lean out the window toward the street and shout, "Jonny, come on in, the food is ready."

When my parents told me the government had turned the house into government property and placed three other families in it free of rent, it made me mad. My father had to fight with the supervisor of housing to allow my grandfather and my aunt to even continue to live there. I could not understand the concept that property could be taken away and now arbitrarily belonged to complete strangers.

Despite the turmoil around us, our home life was almost normal. My brother and I liked pulling pranks on our older sister. Irén was three years older than me and six years older than Istvan and acted as though there was an entire generation between us. We were just children—not in her league. Irén was studying piano at the Academy of Musik, a high school for musically inclined students. My mother was very proud of her, and Irén used that distinction to the hilt. Every time she had to do a chore in the house, she would say she couldn't because she had to practice for her next concert.

One day, Irén declared to the family she had met a very nice boy who wanted to escort her home from school and carry her books. I felt like an outsider was now invading our family. I liked girls but there was no one in school I liked, certainly not enough to carry her books.

One day, our parents were out, and Irén said she was getting ready for a piano lesson, but she had her best dress on. Not only that, she combed her hair for an hour, and put on lipstick and makeup, which was forbidden by Mother. We both knew she was going on a date with that jerk who carried her books. As she was preparing herself, she was giving us orders to do this and do that—things that were otherwise her chores in the house.

Who did she think she was?

We decided to give her a good scare for making us her slaves. I had an idea and set the scene. I got a bottle of tomato juice from the pantry, gave my brother a large kitchen knife and told him, "I'll lie down on the kitchen floor, and you pour the tomato juice on my chest. Put some on the knife so it drips, and then we'll both start screaming and yelling as if I was stabbed with the kitchen knife and the blood will look like it's everywhere. I'll act as if I'm dying."

With my scream, Irén ran out of the bedroom to see what was going on. She took one look at me, began screaming and crying, and fell into a dead faint. Tomato juice got all over her best dress.

Alfred Hitchcock, who I would someday meet, couldn't have done it better.

One positive, albeit somewhat inevitable, development after the incident with Irén was my sudden realization girls were not just playmates like boys. Communism or not, I'd begun to notice they were different somehow—cleaner, better smelling, and with softer skin. That difference began to preoccupy me a great deal. Especially when I thought about certain girls—like Marika.

I met Marika in a Communist summer day camp called "úttörö" (pathfinders). The Communists had these camps in all the Soviet Bloc countries. In the Soviet Union, they were called Pioneers, and were a political copy of the Boys and Girl Scouts. However, there was no gender distinction. All kids were invited to this summer camp in order to recruit kids who hadn't quite been all the way brainwashed at school.

Marika stood out from all the other girls. She always smiled and was very friendly to me. About half the kids wore the Pioneer uniform. I did not. My parents could not afford it, and, even if they could, they wouldn't have allowed me to dress as a Pioneer. Marika not only wore hers every day, but it was always clean and ironed. Her red neckerchief was placed around her neck just right, with the red wooden ring holding it in place.

She looked pleasing in the regulation navy blue skirt, white socks, and new sport sneakers, but her white shirt with two protruding pockets on her chest was something to behold. I had never thought of any girl like that before!

All of a sudden, I didn't care about playing soccer or any other game with any boys. I just wanted to be around and look at Marika.

Our camp was located in a section of the city called the Grand Forest. One day, Marika started into the forest, away from the center of the camp activities. I decided to follow her. At one point when no one could see us, she turned to me and said, "Where are you going?"

I wanted to reply, but no words came out of my mouth.

She said something else, but my ears didn't seem to work either.

After a few seconds, I watched my hand slowly lift, reach out, and gently touch her face. She did not move, but she did blush, which made her look even more beautiful.

We just stood there in silence.

Suddenly, she spun around. Both of her long braids flew, slightly touching my face, as she started running back to the main part of the camp.

I soon noticed there was another boy who seemed to share my interest in Marika. He was a boy I got along with until I realized he was trying to get her attention too. Suddenly, I hated him. My new mission in life was to let him know I was the only one who had the right to her affections. I like to believe I was victorious in that she agreed to let me walk her home when the camp day ended. Even though I knew the detour was going to make me late getting home, and I'd be scolded or punished, I didn't care.

When we arrived at her house, Marika pulled the bell from the street. Her mother came out and was surprised to see her daughter had an escort.

"This is Janos," Marika said, introducing me. "He is in the camp with me and lives this way, so we walked together."

"Oh, where do you live, young man?" she asked.

I lied and told her I lived by a nearby park.

"Why don't you come on in and you two can tell me what happened today in the Pioneer camp."

We followed her inside the house. Marika proceeded to tell her mother all about the camp, omitting anything about our magical encounter in the forest. As she was chattering enthusiastically, I looked around the living room. My eyes froze on framed pictures of Lenin and Stalin. I knew my parents would never have those pictures in our house. Marika's family had to be devoted Communists.

Suddenly, I was uncomfortable being there, and couldn't wait to get home.

Marika and I saw each other at the camp for another month or so. Even though she still filled out her immaculate uniform better than anyone else, my interest in her had withered.

In sixth grade, one of my teachers started an airplane modeling group, and I jumped at the chance to be a part of it. Despite the ravages they'd caused, I remained in awe of the shivering silver bombers flying high in the sky, not to mention the harrowing dogfights of the American, German, and Russian fighters I'd witnessed.

The only problem with the airplane modeling group was we had a total lack of materials to work with. It took the teacher in charge a few weeks, but he found a store in Budapest where the school could acquire the necessary model airplane materials. Unfortunately for the school, there was no money in the school budget to travel to Budapest. The teacher knew our father worked for the railroad, meaning we had free travel on the Hungarian rail systems as family members, so he called us into his office.

The next day, we, two sixth graders, were on our way to the capital with a very special assignment from our school. We felt extremely important and would return as heroes to our teachers, and more importantly, our peers. Budapest was the dream destination for every kid in the country. It had the largest zoo, the permanent Budapest Circus, the largest recreational park with the best rides anywhere, the Hungarian Parliament (the most beautiful building in Europe) and, of course, the Danube. All the other kids were jealous and assumed we would be seeing it all. Never mind seeing all the sights would take at least three days—that is if we ran our way through the city—and we were going there and back in one day.

We got on the early train for the 240 kilometer journey and were in Budapest by 11 a.m. We didn't waste any time finding the airplane model store and searching for everything on our list. We then spent the remainder of the afternoon purchasing packages of balsa wood, glue, and special paper to cover the wings and the fuselage.

We made our way back to the railroad station, which was in the middle of Budapest, an hour before the train left. As we passed an espresso place, I glanced in through the window and spotted one of the biggest film stars in Hungary.

I knew from that day in first grade when my mother volunteered me to recite a poem for the opening ceremony I liked the theater. I'd been scared to death to stand out in front of all those parents, teachers, and kids, but I loved the feeling of all those people listening to what I had to say. The applause afterward was terrific. I knew somehow I would do more performing in front of a crowd at some point, so seeing this old-timer—a star even before the Second World War—was beyond exciting. This actor had became famous for a comedy routine where he came on stage with a bicycle handlebar painted in Communist red and said some funny things about how the new government was steering the country. For this, he was arrested and banned from performing for some time.

Awestruck, my cousin and I stopped and stared at him through the window. After a while, we realized we were being rude, so we walked back and forth in front of the window holding all our airplane modeling material and packages. We did this until we realized we might miss the train back to Debrecen. We had to run at full speed with all our packages toward the railroad station and just made our train. It was worth it to see such a famous person up close.

For seventh and eighth grade, we were sent to Debreceni Református Kollégium or the Reformed College Building. Because the city was the epicenter for the Reformation and Reformed Church in Hungary, they owned the school building. It had a religious and historical presence in the city for centuries and was the site where the new, independent Hungarian Government was formed in 1849. The Communist government closed a lot of churches, synagogues, and historical buildings with notable prewar histories, but they reopened this one for students because they needed the space. My buddies and I felt proud and privileged to attend school in such a place.

The teachers there were exceptional. I remember one of them, Hegedüs Béla, fondly. He was a tall man who was always elegantly dressed. Sometimes, he brought his violin into the classroom and played classical music for us from composers like Liszt Ferenc, Kodály Zoltan, Erkel Ferenc, and others. To his potential peril, he spoke English elegantly and taught us some using his violin. He would have been disciplined or worse if the secretary of the schools found out he was teaching us English folk songs like:

London's burning,
London's burning
Look yonder,
Look yonder
Put on water,
Put on water
London's burning.

English was the language of the enemy, the Western Imperialists, and was not taught in any school in Hungary. Because of this brave teacher and the risks he took, I swore to myself I would someday learn the English language!

I loved to read and always had my nose in the *Count of Monte Cristo* or any book I could trade or borrow from friends. I picked up a few words of English from novels. My favorite books were about cowboys and Indians, and I absolutely loved *The Last of The Mohicans*. Chingachgook became my secret friend from old raggedy books acquired on the black market and passed around from reader to reader, friends, and neighbors. We could not buy them, or any other Western books or newspapers of any kind, because they were not allowed by the government.

I had five or six friends who were also intrigued and inspired by *The Last of the Mohicans*. We loved to discuss the American West and stories about the American Indians.

We would get together between classes and share information on new books we'd heard about, how we might get our hands on them, and decide who got to read them first. Pretty soon, a hierarchy formed among us, and basically, we former our idealized version of a Native American tribe. We were utterly in awe of the culture and decided to meet on a regular basis and display our gear—everything from a crudely fabricated bow and arrow to tomahawks we'd carved out of wood. We made headdresses from turkey and goose feathers. Some of us even had moccasins we'd fashioned ourselves or had made by the local shoemaker (who thought he was making bedroom slippers).

We decided we needed to find a private place where we could conduct our "tribe" business and have our powwows undisturbed, far away from scanning eyes. I remembered an old, abandoned railroad track bordered by forests on both sides that once served a village from our town. It had three oil tanker cars on it that had been there since the war.

One day, after school, I gathered the tribe, and we went to inspect the tankers. One car looked like it had been blown up—it had a big gash and twisted metal protruded from its side as though it had gotten a direct hit from a cannon or a tank. Another looked unharmed but for a series of bullet holes in a straight line toward the top. The third appeared undamaged.

We climbed on top and tried to open the lid of the third tanker, but it would not budge. Having stood there unused for years, it was frozen shut. The tanker with the bullet holes on the sides was our best choice. We climbed on top, and two of us went straight for the lid. It opened easily and we climbed inside. It was clean and did not smell of oil or gasoline. Even though the lid had been closed for many years, the bullet holes had kept the air circulating and the inside was fairly pristine.

We cleaned the inside and drew Native American motifs on the wall of the tanker. We even had a ladder to easily climb in and out. The Braves, as we called ourselves, now had a wigwam made of steel in which to dream of the American West, the adventures of Chingachgook, and the early pioneers.

We were very careful getting in or out to make sure no one saw us so they couldn't report us to the police. Over time, we added a few members to our tribe. First though, we had to make sure the boy, whoever he was, did not have a head full of Communist beliefs and propaganda.

We left our gear, garb, and even our goose and turkey feather head dresses in the steel wigwam. The tanker quickly grew very inviting, and we could not wait to get together in it for our powwows. We started our meetings by lighting up the peace pipe we'd carved based on a photo from a 1930s magazine one of the boys acquired from a family archive.

We sat around and mused about America in general. Most of our families had some kind of radio, which was where we gathered the world news and stories from Radio Free Europe. The program always began with, "This is London calling." My favorite program was *Voice of America.* This was where we got all our international education and news from the other side of the Iron Curtain.

When there was an organized demonstration planned by the city's Communist Party supporting the government or idealizing the Soviet Union, all the students had to gather at school and were given premade signs. We had to shout slogans while marching down our main street in support of government or the glorious Soviet Red Army who freed Hungary from the dreaded the capitalists. At times like this, the Braves stuck together, knowing who we were, and not shouting out the slogans. Sometimes one of us even let out an Indian yell, especially when the teachers were not close by. It was part of the noise of the street, but we felt good about being part of our tribe and not part of the forced show of solidarity, even though we had to be present.

At the end of eighth grade, the time came to think about what was next. I knew my buddies were going to scatter because we had different career goals to pursue.

I wanted to be a mechanical engineer, which made both my parents happy.

"That's wonderful, son," my father said. "Mechanical engineering is a very noble profession. Maybe someday you can own your own airplane. You always wanted to be a pilot."

"That makes me very happy, too," my mother said. "Engineers wear white shirts and ties, just like doctors and lawyers."

My friends and I all had some instinctive knowledge of what we might want to be, but it was not primarily the student nor even their parents who chose what high school to apply to. In fact, our futures were in the hands of the government. This power, of course, filtered down to the local party leaders who made recommendations about who would go to school where. The Communist centralized system was unconcerned about an individual's wishes or choices. They determined how many engineers, chemists, architects etc., the country would produce under a five-year plan and assigned people accordingly.

All the high schools were renamed based on a specific focus, for example Machinery Technical high school or Architectural Technical high school. I intended to register for the Machinery Technical high school because from there I could go to a university and become an engineer. I wasn't alone. A lot of boys coming out of elementary school wanted to study engineering, or at least learn the basics about engineering and then go to the Engineering University.

Surprise, surprise, only the sons of Communist insiders—party secretaries' sons—got into that very popular school. In fact, they'd reached capacity practically before they opened registration, due to prearranged acceptances of kids with the proper parentage. Grades, test scores, and other qualifications be damned. Because my father was not a Communist Party member, I had no chance of getting in.

I was accepted instead into the Bookkeeping Technical high school. I didn't want to be a bookkeeper or an office worker. The only thing I liked about the school was it was in the center of the city. If I wasn't going to be an engineer, I wanted to be an adventurer, entrepreneur, pilot, and skier. I wanted to find my way as an independent person, become somebody as a result of my own effort, see and get to know the world.

I also knew from my experiences under this anything-but-*utopian* society what I wanted to be wasn't what was in store for me. Somehow, I had to change the road I was being sent to travel on.

The Braves met a few times at the steel wigwam during that summer before we all started high school. We all treasured those last meetings. We'd created and established our tribe, not as just a bunch of friends, but with a purpose. We never got caught, but if we had, we could have been thrown out of school or our parents would have suffered the consequences. It was our small rebellion against the political forces intent on taking away our individuality and free will.

Toward the end of the summer, in early August 1951, three of us met up in town. We were sad because we knew this would be the last time we'd discuss tribe business. The others were unavailable because they already had activities associated with their various new high schools.

"What are we going to do with our gear?" I asked.

A sad silence followed.

"I have an idea," I said. "Let's just leave everything where it is! Someday maybe some other kids will find it and take up where we left off."

No one said a word, but we all knew it was exactly the right decision.

We shook hands like adults. At that moment, the Braves became a part of the past and we entered the next phase of our lives.

HIGH SCHOOL

There were three classes of first year students, A, B, and C in the class of 1951. I was happy to have two of my elementary school buddies in Class B with me. One was Sandor and the other was Laszlo. I felt good knowing we'd be together. We'd already known each other for five years, and I had confidence the three of us would look out for each other. Half the class of twenty-eight boys came from peasant stock and took the train from the rural areas surrounding Debrecen. Some lived in the school's dormitory. The rest were local boys including the three of us.

I knew which teachers I liked right from the start: Miss Almády, Mr. Balazsi, and Mr. Erdei. I also knew right away I did not like the principal. She was a short, fat woman who served as the Communist party secretary for the school. The teachers had to abide by her wishes and her wishes came from the party's education ministry.

In high school, there were two groups of students—the first was a small group who believed in Communism with parents who were Communists. These were the students amongst whom the leaders, secretaries, and presidents of the high school youth organizations were selected. They were favored and got better grades.

The others, a majority, were members of the youth organization because we had to be. My friends, the Arpád Téri Csavagók—Tony,

Árpi, Józska, Gondor, Laci, Tisza, Dió, and Hevesi talked among ourselves about the political situation and tried to find answers to certain questions. For example, we were taught *in a Communist country everyone is equal and happy* but even a child could see there was something wrong. Although they told us how wonderful Communism was, we didn't experience it in real life. Every day after school, we had to run to the nearest bakery, grocery, or butcher shop to stand in enormous lines for bread, flour, or meat so the family could eat the next day. There were fights between people who were hungry, frustrated, and had no patience with anyone who tried to get ahead of them in the line. If you went to the railyards however, the freight trains headed eastward were loaded with cars full of beautiful fat pigs, wheat, and brand-new machinery guarded by Russian soldiers with machine guns. We all knew the train's destination was the Soviet Union which begged the question, "Is this the way the glorious Soviet Union is trying to help us?"

One afternoon, I went home, and I found a neighbor crying to my mother because her son had disappeared the previous night.

"Last night there was a knock on the gate. My son went out to see who it was, and he never returned."

Her son had already been taken away once before and served three months in jail for saying the wrong things. I knew of several cases like this all because people tried to exercise freedom of speech.

This time, her son was gone for good.

For that reason, I spent that first year in high school sorting out friends from foes, nerds from brains, and who the whistleblowers were. Once again, we had to join regularly organized propaganda demonstrations along with the other schools and workers, carry signs and praise Communism. The teachers were in charge of keeping a record of who was there and who was not.

Class B was pretty rowdy, especially when the teacher was out of the classroom. A popular pastime was button soccer, which we played on the teacher's podium. All the ardent players had their own button, which was generally large, and often came from an overcoat. The teacher's desk was marked with chalk on both ends to represent the goal area. Each player had to shoot a small button down the field towards the other player's goal with his special button. A shot was made by flicking the large button against the small button, which represented the soccer ball until he got a good shot into the other guy's goal. These games were usually played before class and during the ten o'clock recess between classes.

On one September day in 1953, several boys stood around the button soccer "field" rooting for the players and waiting for their turn to play. The rest of us wandered to our desks awaiting the teacher's arrival.

Suddenly, the door to our classroom opened. A very tall young man walked into the room. He was a bit older than us and looked like he could be a teacher in his fashionable suit, white shirt, and tie. His look defied traditional Hungarian fashion and was very anti-establishment. The suit jacket had a wide lapel, and the pants were very tight on the legs with a high ankle cuff in the new style starting to sweep the country. His shoes had thick, soft soles and were the envy of every young man at the time.

Everyone jumped to their feet as if it were standard procedure. The fellows who were playing soccer quickly cleared the teacher's desk, cleaned off the chalk marks that represented the playing field, and scurried to their seats.

From then on, there was silence, and all eyes were on the well-dressed young man. We assumed he had to be a teacher. That, or some inspector from the government educational office. It was well known the government planted people in factories and other workplaces to inform on people. They let officials know if there were any "enemies of the people" who needed to be dealt with. Children were sometimes urged to turn on their own parents.

The young man stood in the doorway looking at us look at him.

"I am going to be one of you. The principal assigned me to your class," he said. "My name is Sandor Nyiri. Where should I sit?"

We looked at each other until someone finally pointed to an empty spot and said, "No one is sitting there."

As Sandor walked toward his new desk, someone asked, "Where are you from?"

"I am from Szeged, originally," he told us.

Szeged is a beautiful city in the south, close to the Yugoslav border.

"Why didn't you go to school there?"

"That's a long story," he said reluctantly. "And I missed two years of school."

"Why?" I asked.

"Why?" he said with a long sigh and a distinct look of anger. "I was in a concentration camp, together with my family, for all that time."

Suddenly, the school bell sounded marking the start of class for the day. We all were frozen for a second, but soon shuffled over to our seats contemplating what we'd heard from our new classmate.

The teacher came in the class promptly after the bell stopped ringing.

"I didn't hear the usual calamity when I came down the hall, so I thought you all went home," the teacher said. "I hope you've already met your new classmate, Sandor Nyiri."

With that, he started in on the material he was going to teach us for that day. If anything, he treated Sandor with coldness.

I'd heard of the existence of labor camps, which we called concentration camps, but never met anybody who'd been in one. When class was over and the teacher left, we all gathered in front of the class and peppered our new classmate with questions.

"What did you do?" I asked eagerly, wanting to understand.

"Nothing. Picked tomatoes, cabbages, and potatoes under machine gun surveillance," he said, his voice filled with anger. "For free."

"But why did they take you to the camp?"

He looked around. "I'm not supposed to talk about any of this, but we'll be together for another three and half years, so you'll hear it at some point. It might as well be from me and not from hearsay."

"You can trust us," someone else said.

"My father was a military judge in the old Hungarian Army which fought against the Russians, so he was declared an enemy of the people. After the war, he worked on a collective farm because he couldn't get any other kind of job. Although he had a degree in law he was stamped because he had been an officer in the former Hungarian Army.

"The local authorities would harass him sometimes, so we lived in fear that sooner or later they'd come and take him away.

"And then it happened—a bang on the door at midnight. My brother and mother ran to the window, looked out and saw a lot of AVH men surrounding the house.

"When my father went to the door and opened it, the AVH burst in, threw him on the floor, and pointed guns at all of us. Even though we'd always expected it, we couldn't believe it was really happening.

'You're all under arrest!' the officer yelled.

They lined us up at gunpoint and told us we had two hours to gather ur personal belongings. Two AVH men stayed with us, while the officer in charge went away with the rest of the AVH men to give some other poor family the same bad news. At gunpoint, we reluctantly gathered some clothes and little else. The house and everything in it were confiscated and became government property."

We all stood around Sandor quietly. My father had told us that stories like this happened, and we'd all heard whispers, but to us they were just that, stories. This was the first time I'd heard it from someone who'd actually experienced it and lived to tell the story.

Sandor continued. "It was utter chaos in the house. The AVH men watched us like hawks, especially my father. My mother cried the whole time. In the end, they only allowed us to take work clothes, which we had to layer onto our bodies and a small bag of personal stuff like soap and things one would use in daily life. When the AVH man saw me putting the toothbrush in my bag, he smiled and said, 'That won't really be necessary.'

"I heard a truck horn in front of the house.

"'Let's go,' said the AVH men, shoving us out the door.

"The truck doors opened, and two other soldiers came out. There were two more at the back of the truck with machine guns, wearing the round blue cartridge magazine attached to the underside crosswise, hanging from their shoulders. They shoved us onto the truck from the rear. There were a few other families on the truck. The women and small children were crying.

"Two AVH men climbed up with us and the back of the truck door was folded up and secured. There were more stops in the city so additional families could be piled onto the truck. Conversation was forbidden, so it was silent but for the murmur of the engine and the shaking of the truck on bad roads."

"Where did they take you and your family?" someone asked.

"We ended up here, close to Debrecen, on a government farm."

"What did you do on the farm?"

"Fieldwork from dawn to dusk— picking cotton, corn, watermelon, cabbage, or whatever was in season."

"Why didn't you escape when you were in the open field?"

"Because they would shoot you down if you tried to escape."

"And nobody escaped?"

"Some tried and they were punished. Remember we were the *enemy of the people*."

I remember smiling because Sandor certainly did not look like an enemy of anyone.

"How did you live and eat?"

"They cooked for several hundred people, and the cooks were also prisoners like us. We all lived and slept together on cots with hay for a mattress. Over time, we made our environment comfortable as best we could."

"So, how come you are with us now?" someone asked.

"Where did you get that fine outfit?" asked another boy.

We all looked like poor people in patched up clothes, old worn shoes, like gypsies compared to him the way he was dressed.

"Didn't you hear?" Sandor asked.

"Hear what?"

"About Imre Nagy, the new President of Hungary," Sandor said. "He freed all the forced labor and let all the people go from the government farms. We were freed after two and a half years!"

It was 1953, at the peak of the Communist terror and totalitarian regime. The jails and concentration camps were full of political prisoners, people didn't have food or clothing, and many had become restless. The Communists realized this and decided to loosen up a bit. They declared they had gone about some things wrong, and it was the fault of the secretary and the president of the Hungarian communist party, Mr. Rákosi. Suddenly, the hero and number one man in the Communist party disappeared. Everything was blamed on him. Imre Nagy became the President of Hungary. He was a Communist, but a liberal one. After only a few days in office, Nagy became a national hero, mainly because he released all the political prisoners and abolished the concentration camps. He eased taxes on the farmers and he issued an order giving the farmers the right to decide whether they wanted to be in the collective farms or not.

Suddenly there was more food on the market and people who had been forced into labor camps like Sandor and his family were freed.

"My brother was accepted into the Debrecen University. He is studying chemical engineering. I was accepted here at the Bookkeeper Technical High School."

We all absorbed the reality of having this boy who'd been through so much in our midst.

One of my buddies murmured under his breath, "He's probably a whistleblower for the Communist Party."

"Don't say that," I said.

"Oh really, how do you think he got that great outfit?"

On the second day, Sandor came in dressed like the rest of us in old clothes that looked to be secondhand. As it turned out, the suit had been handed down from his brother.

It took a few days before this strange, tall fellow began to blend into our class. Sandor was an intelligent fellow, and it was obvious he came from a good family. He did not come from the proletariat segment of Hungarian society like the rest of us, but had lost everything like all of us just the same. Of course, that made it all the more intriguing to continue to find out more about him and his background.

The new President Imre Nagy lasted for three months before he disappeared from government, not to reappear in any capacity until 1956. He'd implemented a lot of things that were good for the country, like closing the government farms, which was not to the liking of the Soviets occupying the country. A lot of people thought he was killed by the Russians. He was eventually executed along with (Pál) Paul Maléter, the General of the Hungarian Army in 1958 after the Hungarian Revolution against the occupying Soviet Army. In the meantime, the Communists claimed Nagy's government was capitalistic and he was slowly playing the country into the hands of the capitalists.

As our high school years went by, some of my buddies developed into young men who began to conform and accept the dogma being hammered into their brains. Others made the decision to pretend to be Communist to gain recognition and attain their goals—especially when their parents had done the same thing.

Everyone else was growing sick and tired of the Communist regime. They were talking about it in the streets, in the bread lines, and wherever you saw three or four people standing together. Those who were carrying the brightest torch about politics and new ideas, however, were mainly students—high school and university. Slogans like *Rusky Go Home! Where is the freedom of speech? Stop Censorship. Free Press!* were chanted, albeit quietly as it was very dangerous. Student sabotage became popular. Western books began circulating, there was mass *disappearance* from parades, and Communist slogans were torn from walls.

Still, we were fed daily propaganda, often by the principal of the school. She and I never got along, especially after she let my class start a school newspaper and I wrote an objectionable poem in the first edition. Not only was I censored, but almost thrown out of school.

They called my parents and told them I was an agitator, a rebel, an enemy of the people. My mother had to beg and bribe the principal with gifts, so I wasn't expelled. Had they kicked me out, no other school would have taken me because I would have been considered politically dangerous.

"Keep your opinions to yourself and you won't get into trouble," my mother warned me.

As a result of me, the school newspaper lasted only one edition. I was angry, but proud.

I graduated in 1955, having done well in school and placing second in the Hungarian National High School Boxing Championships, but our diplomas weren't complete until we served a so-called "experimental year." This meant the principal assigned each student to a job for a whole year at a small, set salary. Our graduating class was to scatter across the county to different companies in various trades, all of which were government owned. Once the requirement was complete, the graduate either stayed at the position or he could leave and get another job. The real purpose of this law was to supply certain governmental agencies that didn't have enough help—or where nobody wanted to work—with labor.

I was assigned to a small-town agricultural collection office in charge of keeping track of the local farmers. Each farmer was assigned a predetermined number of crops to grow and turn over to the government. If they didn't comply or they didn't meet their quota because of a poor growing season, they then owed it to the government in future crops. My job, along with several other office workers, was to figure out from a government chart precisely how much each farmer had to give to the government and how much they could keep for their families. More than half the farmers on whom I kept files owed two to three years' worth of back crops and animals to the government. In some cases, once I figured out what was owed, the farmer had almost nothing left on which to live.

From my first day on the job, farmers came in to beg us to let their debt go. I couldn't stand listening because I couldn't do anything for them. I tried to make excuses to leave when I could. Then, I began to make deliberate mistakes in favor of the farmers.

One day, a farmer came into my office to complain about how high his agricultural taxes were and he couldn't pay. He asked me if I would let some of his dues go. I told him I had no power to do that, because all I did was figure out numbers on the basis of a chart formulated by the ministry of agriculture. He still said he would appreciate anything I could do for him and took out a bottle of wine from his bag and put it on my desk. At that moment, my manager walked in. At first, I thought they had rigged the scenario to see whether I would favor the farmer or not. Then, the police were called, and the farmer was thrown out.

Nevertheless, I was assigned to the field for two weeks as a penalty simply for listening to this poor man's complaints about being a "modern slave."

The next morning, the manager came to me and gave me the address and a list of crops a particular farmer owed to the government. "You and your fellow comrade will go and confiscate whatever crops and animals you find. This man is a 'Kulák.' He doesn't want to serve the government his duty and he is obligated to do so."

I'd definitely heard stories like this, and I'd certainly been on the receiving end of marauding Russian soldiers, but I had never been part of anything like this.

"By the way," the manager continued. "Before you go out, sign this paper. It's mandatory."

"What is it?" I asked.

"This will authorize us to deduct eighty percent of your salary as a Peace Loan to the Hungarian Government."

I heard his words, but I certainly did not fully understand what I was signing was a contribution, not a loan, that was supposed to bring me *personal* peace. I definitely felt uneasy, but it wasn't as though I had a choice.

We got on the horse wagon and went to the address provided to retrieve the crops the farmer was allegedly hiding from the government. When we arrived, my colleague opened the big gate so the horse wagon could get in. He didn't so much as say hello to the farmer or his family. When we were inside, he locked the gate. The farmer just stood there, dread on his face, knowing what would happen next.

We entered the house, his wife in a dark corner, crying.

We sat down at a table and my colleague proceeded to read to the farmer what he owed to the government.

"Yes," the farmer admitted readily. "But I don't have anything left. We already gave everything we had. There is nothing left to give."

"But you did not fulfill your obligation."

"Please understand, there is nothing left but a few chickens in the yard."

"Go out and look around," my colleague instructed me. "See what they have."

I did as I was told, my head spinning. I counted a dozen chickens and a few geese but no other animals.

My colleague came out with the farmer and his sobbing wife.

"Please don't do this," she said. "We have nothing else to give."

"You did not satisfy your allotment to the government."

After twenty minutes of pointless arguing, my colleague turned to me and said, "Let's go catch those chickens and take them."

I was flabbergasted.

"We are going to starve this winter," the farmer said.

His wife sobbed harder.

"The proletariat in the city also has to eat. Work harder and fulfill your obligations to the people, to the workers of this country."

I thought of my grandfather, father, and the neighbor's son, the concentration camps, the slogans, and the parades. I recalled how my whole family stood at gunpoint while they were beating my grandfather to death. How often had our livestock been taken from us?

"No," I said, horrified, and thinking about the rabbits and geese stolen from us. "These people won't have anything to eat."

With that, I got back on the wagon, refusing to take the last few pairs of chickens and geese these poor people had. I went back to the office, gave the files to the manager, and told him I was leaving.

He started to say something, but I didn't wait for him to finish.

As I gathered my belongings, the office workers stood there watching me in shock.

"Don't do this," one said. "You won't be able to get another job."

"Remember you are on probation and in training from your school," another said.

I was convinced this job had been assigned to teach me a lesson or reform me since the principal of my school knew I had not been properly brainwashed into Communist Utopian beliefs. By doing this work, they thought I would be taught the benefits of Communism and learn everything should and did belong to the people.

I couldn't find the right words to say, instead, I knocked over a seat in anger. Then, I walked to the railroad station and went back to Debrecen.

"What's going to happen now? Nobody is going to hire you. You will be lucky to get a laborer's job!" My mother said angrily when I showed up at home.

My sisters and my brother just stood there not really knowing how to react to my story.

However, when I glanced over at my father, he stood there listening with a slight smile. "Now you have had a taste of what I was talking about when I tried to explain the truth of our precious Communists, and their *everything belongs to the people* dogma. They never say the other half is just starving to death."

A few days later, I got my diploma in the mail. It read, "Experimental year" Started . . . then the date, with the Government Agricultural Collection agency stamp below and the word, "Disqualified."

I'd basically forfeited my high school diploma and my action had effectively ended my ambition to go to a university. My future was entirely derailed, not that I was sure I had one after experiencing this incredible but commonplace injustice. The incident was put in my personal ID book, which had to be carried at all times and shown when one applied for a job or for any reason— for example when the police wanted to identify you.

I was proud of myself for what I'd done, but what was my future going to look like, especially with such a big mark in my personal ID book? I still wanted to be an engineer, and a pilot, and an actor, but I also wanted to be an inventor and an entrepreneur. And then there was my dream to travel all over the world—eventually landing in the American West. There had to be a way to create the life I wanted, but it seemed impossible.

ALL THE WORLD'S A STAGE

After a few weeks of lingering without a job and far too much time to contemplate my lack of future, my father was able to use his railroad connections to get me a low-level position with the railway support division of the railroad.

When I was in school, we went down into a coal mine. The men worked like animals, throwing the coal into the lorry with enormous shovels all day along. While I was down there, all I could think about was designing a coal mine that wouldn't be as devastating to work in. My new job was the above-ground equivalent. The work consisted of two people facing each other on one rail and two men doing the same on the other rail. All held very heavy picks, sharp on one end with a solid piece of steel and like a hammer on the other. In rhythm, we packed granite pieces under the railroad ties to keep the rails straight and strong.

To do that task eight hours per day can only be described as torture. Most of the men I worked with on this brigade came from the country and nearby villages. Although they were considered to be from the bottom rung of society, they were strong people who had no choice but to do this job because the government had confiscated their land. They were no longer farmers but laborers working for next to no money. These were people who worked hard with their hands—in other words, they were the typical proletariat.

I was the only city boy on the crew.

The old man who served as crew master didn't do any physical work, he just constantly harassed us to hurry up. "How will we meet our daily requirement if you guys are this slow?"

On his lapel, he wore both the Hungarian and Communist red flag emblems.

No one paid much attention to him—just enough so he didn't report us and get us fired.

Whenever I allowed myself to daydream, I found I longed to be an actor.

"Actors live an immoral life," my mother would say when I mentioned it.

Her attitude made no sense to me because she was always taking us to the theater, especially when the program was an operetta. She loved musicals and had a flair for the theater. She knew I did too.

The Communist leadership had started up a theater in Debrecen. The thinking was aspiring young actors could become educated through theater—in other words, brainwashed. Because there were many small towns in the countryside where they could perform plays written by the government for the peasants, it was a winning proposition all around.

The Csokonai theater was built in 1865 and had survived both wars. One of the small rehearsal halls across the street was called the Stanislavsky Theater. It was named for the Russian theater personality who wrote the book called, *How the Actor Prepares,* which became the basis for Method Acting in 1930s New York.

I got the opportunity to train at the Stanislavsky theater as an amateur. The theatre had no seats, it was just a place where we could rehearse. We were all amateurs, so it was a privilege to have some famous actors from the big Csokonai theater direct and teach. We performed plays chosen by the Communist cultural propagandists and the basic storylines were almost always the same: poor peasant boy whose family was devastated by big landowners succeeds in getting the beautiful daughter of the landowner to marry him and show the audience the real winners are the peasants and the proletariat.

In spite of the political dogma, I loved being on stage. It made the hard labor I had to endure during the day almost bearable.

I loved the theater and had begun to think it was an ambition I might be able to realize, so I put in an application for the Theater and Film Art University in Budapest and prayed for a miracle.

I was delighted when I received an application complete with a two-page questionnaire. I also had to include a detailed biography.

A few weeks later, I got a letter in the mail. My application had been reviewed and I was invited to come try out with instructions to learn a poem of my choice to recite on stage.

I read the letter over and over again for days until I'd calmed down enough to find a poem and start rehearsing.

On the appointed day, I caught the early train to Budapest and arrived well ahead of my audition at the university. With time to spare, I walked over to the side of the Danube, close to the beautiful Hungarian Parliament, and searched for a quiet spot on the riverbank where I could rehearse my poem a few final times. As I got just below Parliament, someone yelled in my direction. I looked around but didn't see anyone. The yelling continued. Suddenly, three soldiers appeared with machine guns, all pointing at me.

"This is a restricted area!"

Terrified, I turned back and walked the other way as quickly as I could and kept going for nearly a kilometer before I dared to stop again. This time, I went down until I was three steps from the water and sat down to rehearse my poem.

Despite my earlier scare, I was sleepy from the early morning train ride and apparently dozed off. The rising tide of the Danube, cold and wet at my feet, awakened me just in time to get to my audition.

A guard checked me in and sent me up to the second floor theater. At the backstage door, they checked me in again, told me to have a seat, and said they'd call me when it was my turn. The room was large and full of people and a young man was on stage reciting his poem. I looked around in the audience, some looked familiar. As it turned out, they were recognizable actors I'd seen in movies who'd come to observe new kids like me.

My legs shook as two more brave souls were called onto the stage, recited their poems, and were told they'd be notified by mail.

Finally, my name was called.

"Go to stage center," a teacher said from behind me. "Introduce yourself, the title of the poem, and the name of the poet."

I felt like I was walking toward my execution as I started onto the stage, looked into the audience, and saw even more faces I recognized from theater and film.

I was just as nervous about performing as I had been after my mother volunteered me to recite a poem in first grade. On that day, as I stood facing the crowd full of kids and parents, I looked at my mother and saw her pointing skyward.

I wished my mother were there to give me courage through her sign language, but I knew I better do what I'd come here for.

I began to recite my poem.

As a first grader, there was thunderous applause when I finished. I even remember hearing some whistles. I saw my mother bending over a little. I knew what that meant, and I did too. They clapped even more.

There was no applause for my audition poem.

"Good," someone in the audience simply said. "We'll inform you of the next steps by mail."

I assumed I was a disaster.

When I returned home that day my mother moved around the house with frenetic excitement. She tried to keep her curiosity under control, but finally asked, "How was it?"

"They are going to send a letter."

"Ah," she said pretending to be disinterested.

Nothing more was said.

Two weeks later, a letter arrived asking me to return to the university. I was to be assigned a student director who would work with me on the poem, and I would recite it once again.

"They liked you!" my mother said. "I just knew they would."

On the assigned date, I met with a senior student who worked with me on the poem. After twenty minutes with the student director, I did my poem again on the same stage.

"We'll notify you by mail," I was told once again.

A few weeks later, a letter arrived inviting me to the university a third time. For this callback I would be given a three-minute scene and assigned a senior student director to work with. I would then perform that scene as a final audition. Afterward, I would be notified by mail if I was accepted to the university.

I sailed through the process, loving every moment.

Over three weeks passed before the final letter came. The essence of the notification was, simply, "You were not accepted because you are not politically desirous."

I was devastated by the realization of what had happened. All through that summer, while I was trying out, the Communist arm of the university was checking me out. They knew my father had refused to join the party repeatedly, and they knew all about my ten-day post-high-school career. The teachers wanted me, but the Communist Party was determined to punish me.

I was nineteen years old. I wanted to be an actor. I also wanted to be an entrepreneur and an inventor. If I failed, I wanted to do so because of my own inabilities, not roadblocks set up based on my refusal to believe what I was being told to think. I had such big dreams, but the only thing I knew for sure was in the world where I lived, my future would add up to little or nothing.

Sadly, my situation wasn't any worse or better than most others in the country.

REVOLUTION

By 1956, there was a large Soviet occupational force in Hungary, enough to not only control our country, but eventually take the rest of Europe, and defend themselves in case of Western attack. The Russian officers had moved their families to Hungary. They shopped in special grocery stores that were always full of food while we waited in long lines for what little was on the store shelves.

Simmering tensions began to boil. People began to speak more freely, sometimes even loudly cussing the Russians. Of course, radio shows like the *Voice of America* and the British Broadcasting Corporation helped spread the word.

In Budapest, the Petofi Circle, an organization made up mainly of students, artists, and intellectuals was formed. As Revisionist Communists, their goal was to bring Imre Nagy back. Meetings were held that were daring and critical of the current regime. Speakers were arrested, but others took their places.

Tensions continued to mount.

During the first half of October, more and more people were having heated political discussions in public places. Security police and regular police began to patrol in greater numbers.

The Hungarian Communist Party and the government sent a delegation to Yugoslavia for the first time since they broke away from the Soviet Bloc.

"We are going to be friends with Yugoslavia in spite of Russia," I heard someone say out loud at a coffee shop.

"Why don't the Russians get out of Hungary like they promised several years ago?" someone else asked.

On October 23rd, 1956, there were demonstrations against the Russians, demanding democratic reforms of free press, free radio, an end to collective farming, and the withdrawal of troops. It was peaceful, but there were some arrests.

I was rehearsing at the theater, occasionally running out to observe the events. I noted there were increasingly more people in the streets. At two and three in the afternoon, the schools and universities let out. At five and six, factory and office workers joined the already growing crowd. We finally stopped working and left the theater. Each person was like a drop of gasoline in a boiling tank ready to blow at any moment. I was one of those people that evening, just walking and waiting around for something big, exciting, and dangerous. What we really were waiting for was revenge.

I went into the nearest store and bought ten yards of red, white, and green ribbon—the Hungarian national colors used by rebels in the much-revered Revolution of 1848. I cut it into short pieces to give out to people. I put one of these ribbons on my left upper arm. It was a great feeling to see security police come by and notice the ribbon on my arm, knowing they wanted to arrest me, but they wouldn't get out of the crowd alive if they did.

As it grew darker, the crowd became increasingly restless. There were no more security police or Russians in the streets because they knew their presence would not help bring about peace. Only city police were in evidence, but they were well known anti-Communists. People were discussing the news and we all knew there were demonstrations in every major city in the country.

By the time night fell, there were two major gatherings—one at City Hall, which was surrounded by security police, and another in front of the newspaper building, which was also surrounded but with city police. I ran back and forth between the two buildings observing. I spotted a car coming from the direction of the university. It had a large three-color flag affixed to the side and a student sitting on top yelling, "Let's go to the publishing house to publish a declaration from the university students. We want to publish it so everybody can read it."

We joined up by jumping onto the hood of the car.

"Make way and follow us; we're going to the publishing house to publish a declaration!" The student and I waved the declaration at the crowds as we approached the press building.

The crowd there was enormous.

"Read it!" and "Let's hear it!" they yelled.

We ran with a copy to the top of the stairs and shouted out the contents:

"This is a ten-point declaration put together by the students at the university. We intend to publish it in the papers tonight. Point One: We demand that the Russian Army units leave Hungary immediately. Two: We demand a multi-party system. Three: Abolish collective farming . . ."

111

As I continued to read all ten points, the crowd roared in approval and shouted, "Down with Communism!"

The ten points had been printed on a single page that was given out to the people.

This action resulted in an invitation to discuss these points in front of the university. A loudspeaker was soon set up in the park, which was already full of students. People kept coming from all directions.

A professor began to speak but was interrupted by several students running out of the building yelling, "The Revolution has broken out in Budapest! There is open fighting going on between the students and the security police."

Flags were brought out of the building and given away. We cut out the Communist emblem leaving a big hole in the center of the flag. We marched in a loose formation filling the street toward City Hall, singing the Hungarian national anthem as we went. There were students, workers, farmers, professors, men, and women. I looked back but I couldn't see the end of the crowd —this, in my home-town—I thought, proudly.

We were halfway to City Hall when we encountered a roadblock of ten city policemen.

The sergeant shouted toward the oncoming crowd, "You can't enter this area. We have orders to stop you."

We marched right through their line. Some of the police even joined the crowd. The security police began shooting into the air in an attempt to scare people away, but it only worked temporarily because we got there, still in formation, and singing revolutionary songs. The people who had run off into the side streets from the sound of gunfire joined us again.

No one, nothing, could stop this crowd.

Suddenly, the citywide loudspeakers controlled by City Hall were turned on: "Dear Comrades, don't let yourself be influenced by groups of fascists and by a small mob! Go home! Leave the streets!"

In front of us, a double line of security police shot into the air and shouted at us to not come any closer.

We came closer and closer anyway.

They began to throw tear-gas bombs.

Temporarily blinded, my eyes burning, and bullets whizzing by, I ran into the hallway of a house with several other people. When I could see again, there was no one around me. I heard the sound of gunfights and ran out to people running and screaming.

As I stood on the sidewalk, frozen and not knowing what to do, machine gunfire erupted from the attic windows of the Paul Beer Parlor and Restaurant. I threw myself to the ground as bullets struck the wall above me where I'd been standing. Plaster rained down on me. I crawled back to the hallway and looked out, helpless to do anything. There was chaos on the streets.

There were rumors that soldiers were giving away guns from an army truck a few blocks away. The shooting stopped, but the crowd refused to disappear until after midnight.

The freedom fight was on.

The next day the Revolutionary City Government was formed. My favorite teacher, Erdeii Gabor, from high school became part of it.

Despite the fact that the Russian Air Force base was just outside of the city, they did not interfere with the Revolutionary government and its forces. We did not interfere with them. That agreement might have been the first action of the new government in my city, Debrecen.

Debrecen had been won, but in many cities, the fighting was still going on.

In Budapest, there was an actual war developing between the Russian forces and the civilian revolutionary with help from the Hungarian Army and police who sided with the Revolution. AVH stations were overtaken. Horrible interrogation chambers were discovered and some of the brutal Hungarian security forces were hung on the street.

Political prisoners were freed.

Finally, the Revolution was won all over the country.

Cardinal Mindszenty was freed and Imre Nagy became president again.

The Nagy government called for the withdrawal of Soviet Occupation forces and did away with Hungary's commitments to the Warsaw Pact. It declared Hungary a neutral and sovereign state that wished to be at peace with all its neighbors, including the Soviet Union. The Russians even began to negotiate for the peaceful return of Hungary to the Hungarian people.

Hungary was free!

RAILROADED

The morning after the fighting in Debrecen, while the Revolution raged on in Budapest, I arrived at the building in the rail complex where we gathered at the start of every day. Excitement, worry, and uncertainty filled the air. Some people were afraid to talk about the Revolution for fear that it was not really happening. Any talk of overthrowing or going against the government—not to mention the Russians—was terrifying. But others, including me, were trying to figure out what to do— how to apply ourselves in the face of this news and rumors of a national strike.

We needed a leader from amongst our group of fourteen who could organize and strategize. Surprisingly, a fellow worker who was never an agitator or leader type but more hard working with a good personality, began to assert himself into the cavalcade of conversation.

"What can we do to show our solidarity?"

"We don't know how the city of Debrecen is going to react to this news. Certainly, we don't know how our own railroad leadership will align themselves," he said. "We can see all rail traffic is at a standstill. That should give us the idea that the whole country, at least the Hungarian railroad organization, sympathizes with the Revolution."

In truth, we didn't know anything for sure.

"I have a suggestion," I said. "Why don't we choose a delegation, maybe two or three people . . ."

Before I could finish my sentence, someone yelled, "There's a freight train of six cars arriving on one of the rails from Budapest. It doesn't seem to be slowing down or stopping."

We all ran out in time to watch the six-car train pass by our building. A Russian soldier holding a machine gun was perched on each corner of every car. We heard Hungarian words from inside the freight cars and saw hands reaching out of the small window openings. They were prisoners captured by the Russians in Budapest. We just stood there, stunned, knowing the train was headed east and wouldn't stop until it reached Russia.

"We've got to do something," more than one of us said.

"But what? We cannot attack the train. We don't have any guns. Even if we try, the Russians will mow us down."

"Let's get inside," said Joe, our newfound leader. "I have an idea."

When we were safely inside and out of earshot he said, "Let's choose two of us to go to town, see what is happening there, and check in with the railroad administration office for information and instructions."

We all agreed this was the best course of action.

Several of us volunteered, but Joe chose me. Later, he told me I was his choice because I was the only one who had graduated from high school.

I noticed our group leader, who was in his railroad uniform, did not get involved in any of this. I also realized the Communist flag emblem was not on his lapel, where it had always been. He had absolute power over everyone in the group and our work assignments for the day, but Comrade Group Leader was quiet for once. He knew he would not get any support from anyone if we turned on him.

At 8:00 a.m., Joe and I set out for town and into the railroad track manager's office to determine where things stood. The people who worked in this office were career, high-ranking officers of the Hungarian railroad. To be in this kind of leadership/managerial position, they had to be in the Communist party. But since the railroad was a national entity, we knew they knew a lot more than we did about the situation in the country. Normally, laborers were not allowed in their domain, much less permitted to discuss anything with them. These were unique circumstances, however. Besides, there would be no security at the main entrance to turn us away.

The few people in the building we encountered looked at us strangely because we weren't wearing proper uniforms. Still, they pointed us to the main office.

We knocked, went inside, and greeted three high-ranking railroad officers by saying, "Good morning," and not the proper Communist, "Freedom Comrades," as was the new custom.

Two of them returned our greeting the old-fashioned way. Only one said, "Szabadsag Comerads."

The two who greeted us with, "Good morning," glanced at each other simultaneously, and with surprise.

The one officer who must have been the Communist Party secretary opened a drawer and placed his hand on what we assumed was a revolver. He wanted us to know in case we'd come with guns of our own and meaning harm. Of course we hadn't, but his hand remained there while we told them we were rail workers from VIII Railroad Track Service division and were there to find out what they, the management, knew and recommended as to how we should proceed.

No one spoke.

"We don't know," one of the men finally said. "We are waiting for instructions from the ministerium ourselves."

"Rumor says there will be a national strike," said the other officer. "As a matter of fact, the Hungarian railroad is now at a standstill."

I told them about the small freight train we'd seen two hours earlier carting prisoners toward Russia from the Revolution in Budapest, complete with machine gun toting soldiers hanging on every corner. I told them we even heard female voices from the cars.

"There is no other train movement on the tracks throughout the system," they said. "We're going to have to wait until things straighten out in Budapest and we hear from railroad headquarters for instructions."

"We'll go back to the workers and tell everyone to go home then," I said.

"What is the motivation of the workers?" asked the comrade, speaking for the first time. "What are they saying? How do they feel?"

"Everyone wants the Russians to leave Hungary immediately."

"Would they fight if it comes to that?"

"Yes," I said, adding, "I know I would. We want a free Hungary without Communism and the Russians."

"So far, the Russians are staying on their bases in Debrecen. There is no movement, at least not that we can see from our gathering place at the railroad station next to the steam engine terminal," Joe said.

"I wish they would pack up and leave without any bloodshed like they were supposed to in 1947," I said.

With that, we said our goodbyes, turned, and walked out of the building.

We went back and told everyone what happened, what was said, and everyone could go home.

"Wait a minute," said our official group leader, finally speaking up. "I am in charge here, and it is still working hours. You have to stay until I say you can go!"

We ignored his orders and went on our way.

We were now strikers, taking matters into our own hands. The old man was left alone, looking like a horse soldier without a mount.

The Soviet Union announced they were going to withdraw all their forces from Hungary and would send new forces to assure the safe withdrawal of their divisions from Hungary, but we knew better than to believe them.

In Budapest, Imre Nagy and General Malter Pal were invited to discuss the withdrawal of the Soviet troops.

They went and never returned.

On November 4, 1956, just before daybreak, the Russian invasion began all over the country. We didn't have arms and ammunition, we lacked manpower, and we couldn't fight alone against tanks and airplanes. Still, the Freedom Fighters in Budapest staged a valiant defense.

In Debrecen we formed small individual groups even though we knew we could never win again. We did spot fighting during the night, attacking small Russian units, cutting telephone wires, etc. There was a big water tower that supplied the city, so we went up there because it was higher than anything else and we saw our whole town surrounded by tanks.

Budapest fell, and the 1956 Hungarian Freedom Fight was over. The Communists came out of hiding and took power again. Blood-thirsty, power-hungry, Janos Kadar was installed as president and the Communist revenge began. Thousands of Freedom Fighters were killed or sent to Soviet work camps. Some 5000 Hungarians went to the gallows or faced firing squads in the aftermath.

Hungary had been free for only five days.

ON THE RUN

I met up with my brother Istvan one evening to walk home from work together. Halfway to the house, we encountered four Russian tanks headed in our direction. All four trained their headlights on us as they passed us. One tank pulled out of the line and came directly at us.

"Keep cool," I said.

"I am," my brother said. "Act like you're not afraid at all."

"I'm trying," I said.

We knew the Russians wanted to see if we were armed and then scare us either way. When we didn't react at all, the tank quickly pulled back in line and the four-tank column went on its way toward the city center.

When we arrived home, my father pulled me aside about something even scarier. "I was informed by one of my colleagues that your name came up at the railroad track service office. You are at risk of being interrogated or punished because of your behavior when the *forradalome* broke out." He paused. "He also recommended you get away from here."

Many intense discussions followed.

It was decided I needed to leave Hungary for my own safety. Like me, my good friend Tony's name had also come up, so he would join me. He had an aunt and uncle in the United States, so we decided that would be our ultimate destination. The conversation spread to my closest friends, a lot of whom feared for their safety and future, as well. They would also join us.

Istvan wanted to come as well.

"He is just a child. Don't take him," my mother begged.

I did not want to leave my brother behind, but I didn't know how dangerous the escape would be and I couldn't bear the idea of anything happening to him, so it was decided he would stay behind. Irén was married by this time, so Tony and I went to her house to find out whether she and her husband would come with us. We talked all day and night, and into the next dawn. They decided not to come along because they had a one-year-old baby, Zsuzsika.

Their choice would prove wise.

Tony and I met at 7:00 a.m. on the appointed day at a particular corner on Samsoni Road. We took the streetcar to Apafa Street where we got off to meet up with our friends. Our plan was to get back on and embark on our perilous journey emboldened by our closest friends.

When we got to Apafa Street and got off the streetcar however, no one was there. We waited for the second streetcar to come, and still no one showed up. With no other choice, we got back on the streetcar and proceeded, just the two of us. We would later find out one of our friends told his parents about the secret plan. They called around and the rest of our friends had been quarantined by their parents who would not let them go because of the many dangers inherent in crossing the Austrian-Hungarian border.

Not to mention the unknown, which lay beyond . . .

Tony and I got off the streetcar and started down the main street toward Nagy Allomas, our equivalent of Grand Central Station, or what had been rebuilt of it after it had been devastated in the bombing I'd witnessed from my great uncle's farm on the hill.

We approached a corner but stopped about 100 yards back when I spotted a cannon from a Russian tank protruding into the street. Because we were dressed like a railroad worker and a laborer, we decided it was safer to go the back way on small streets and through the freight yards between the rail cars. This was the first of what would be many smart decisions necessary to evade the enemy on our path to freedom.

There were no trains when we got to the station, so we had to wait there for almost three hours. When the train finally arrived, people crowded on, shoulder to shoulder, most of them wanting to get out of the country. Tony wanted to go inside the railroad car, but I said no. If a train slowed and we needed to get off for any reason we could easily disappear from the railroad car's platform. This turned out to be a good strategy, which we would employ more than once.

The train stopped at Szolnok, a city of 200,000, halfway to Budapest. We spotted AVH and other men on the side of the station building. They had guns and were coming aboard. I signaled Tony to get off the train on the side facing the yard. We hid in the shadow of the freight cars and ran forward to where the train would come when it started again. When it was time, we jumped onto a different car.

Riding along with us in the new car were two uniformed Hungarian Air Force officers. They had no decoration or rank displayed on their shoulder.

"Where are you going?" I asked.

"Budapest," one of them said briskly, obviously not wanting to talk.

"Are you officers?"

"Yes."

"You don't have your insignias on."

"We took them off."

"Are you still in the Air Force?"

"Yes," one of them said.

I realized they were going to join their Hungarian army in Budapest to fight but they didn't want to discuss it.

The train finally pulled into the Western station at the end of the line in the center of Budapest. From there, we had to head to the other side of the city to get to the South train station. Unfortunately, there were no streetcars due to the widespread devastation and destruction caused by the battle between the Russians and the Freedom Fighters—more even than there had been during the war.

We crossed the Danube and arrived at the park close to the South railroad station. Walking through, we spotted many dead bodies covered in lime to disinfect them. Suddenly, Russian soldiers in tanks and other equipment coalesced in front of a nearby four-story apartment building. Shots were fired inside and the Russians rushed the building. Under different circumstances we would have wanted to know what was going on and how it ended, but we couldn't have been more anxious to get out of there and get to our destination.

Once again, there was no train when we arrived.

Several hours later, we boarded a train headed in the general direction of the Austrian border. Like our last train, it was full of people who wanted to defect.

In his pocket, Tony had a piece of paper with the address of an aunt who lived with her family in Detroit, Michigan, USA.

"We need to memorize the address and destroy the paper," Tony said. "If the Russians or the AVH find this, we are doomed."

I still know the address to this day:

7755 Osage Street

Detroit, Michigan, USA.

While Tony had family waiting to greet him in the USA, I had relatives who lived along our route to safety. I did not know if the train would stop anywhere near them, but as it was slowing down at Érdliget, I came up with a strategy. We would get off the train and stay for a few days with my Uncle Istvan and Aunt Juliska— relatives on my mother's side—so the reasons for our trip would not seem so obvious. In addition, we were now on the western side of Hungary and didn't know our way around, so they could help direct us as to which way to go.

My aunt and uncle greeted us with open arms—housing us, feeding us, and making us feel at home. We did not tell them about our plans, but they knew and we learned a lot from them. They knew people and had information, good, bad, and otherwise as to what was happening at the border of Hungary and Austria. The most important thing we learned was there really was no safe route. The trains were not running with any regularity, and we couldn't count on any particular transportation.

"Don't risk your lives," they said. "Go back to Debrecen."

We were at greater risk by going home. Even if we weren't in imminent danger of harassment or arrest, we had no future whatsoever. After all, my aunt and uncle had owned a small movie house in Erd Lioget village, which the government had taken away from them. Just to rub it in, they were forced to be employees in the business they'd devoted their lives to building. What would become of Tony and I who were already under scrutiny?

After three days, my uncle heard a train was coming through that evening. It was headed to Székesfehérvár, a city southwest of Budapest. The border was still a long way away, but it got us closer to our goal.

We said our goodbyes, thanked my aunt and uncle for their hospitality, and caught this train.

We arrived in Székesfehérvár at 1:00 p.m. the next day and found ourselves in a passenger waiting room full of hopeful defectors. The newspaper stand was open. I went to check it out and saw two interesting books. Having zero previous experience escaping a country, I figured I'd buy them so that when the AVH or the Russians came, we would just pretend to read, and they wouldn't bother us. One book,

The Storm Over Italy, would remain in my possession for the next thirty years. I gave the other book to Tony.

There was no sign of another train, and no one knew if or when another would be coming. Just past midnight, there was rustling, movement, and speech that didn't make sense. Tension permeated the air. Sure enough, three policemen, AVH, and soldiers entered looking for people to arrest. It was clear pretending to read books wouldn't do a bit of good. Luckily, Tony and I were at the other end of the waiting room near a door. I gave him a signal and we snuck out onto the unfamiliar streets of Székesfehérvár. We walked all night and into the early morning, never going far from the rail station and hiding when necessary from military vehicles and personnel.

After observing the comings and goings at the station carefully, and sure there were no more unwanted government authorities or Russians lurking about, we found out a train heading for the Austrian-Hungarian border would be leaving late that afternoon. It was a slow train headed in a southwesterly direction, stopping at all stations. We didn't care, as long it took us closer to the border.

We boarded with no problem.

The trip was blissfully boring and entirely uneventful. It was nearly 3:00 a.m. when we reached the train's final destination. We did not know the name of the town or how far from the border it actually was. We did not go into the station for fear of being questioned. Instead, we lurked in the pitch dark near the platform where we thought no one would pay any attention to us.

Suddenly, a railroad worker approached.

"Can I help?" he asked.

I didn't know what to say or if I should say anything at all. However, he understood exactly why we were standing there in the middle of the cold dark night.

"Are you trying to reach the border?" he asked. Without waiting for an answer from us he continued, "If that's the case, your best bet is to go this way." He pointed straight across the tracks. "You will see a narrow-gauge track and a small railroad station. There should be a train going to Répcevis. It's a small village but the border is about two or three kilometers from there."

"Thank you," Tony and I said, dumbfounded by his kindness.

"Nothing to it, boys," he said. "Sorry to see you go."

With that, the man walked away.

We crossed the tracks and, sure enough, there was a narrow-gauge track with a train consisting of three cars and a small steam engine. We climbed aboard the last car. The train was already nearly full of people—adults, children, teenagers, and whole families all attempting to leave Hungary. Soon, the mini-steam engine began to move, we hoped, toward Répcevis.

Around 7:00 a.m., we heard someone say we were getting close. We did not know what to expect and something felt off to me about a train full of people all trying to escape Hungary. We weren't sure what we should do. It seemed risky to go into the small station with all these people who were clearly refugees.

"We have to jump off the train before it pulls into the station," I told Tony.

"Jump off?" Tony asked.

"Yes," I said. "I think it's our best chance."

The train slowed. I looked ahead and saw the homes on the out-skirts of Répcevis come into view.

"Now!" I said.

Without hesitation, I opened the car's door and jumped. Tony followed.

We landed safely with no injuries and laid low by the tracks, can-vassing the nearby houses and backyards while we watched that train pull into the station.

We wondered how our fellow travelers fared but didn't dare ap-proach the station to find out.

THE FARMER AND HIS WIFE

There was a small gate at the first house by the railroad track. I looked around and confirmed no one had witnessed our leap from the moving train. We noticed there was a small barn nearby, so we proceeded to sneak over and open the little backyard gate. We opened the barn door, went in, and introduced ourselves to the two cows inside. It had been two days since we'd slept, so we made a place in the hay and promptly dozed off.

We were awakened mid-afternoon by banging on the door. I had been sleeping deeply and I didn't know where I was for a few seconds.

"I know you're in there," a voice said, the banging on the door growing louder.

I went from sound asleep to utterly terrified.

"Don't worry. You are safe with us, but I need to know if you have guns."

"No," I finally said. "No . . . guns!"

"Okay, then. I'm coming in. Don't be afraid."

With that, the barn door opened and an older, heavyset farmer came in carrying a tray of fresh bread and warm milk. He had a kindly smile.

"I knew you were in here and wanted you to rest a little before I disturbed you. You need to stay in here while it is daylight, but once it is dark, I welcome you to come into the house. We'll put you up in the attic, give you something good to eat, and discuss how we can help you further."

It was one of the happiest outcomes I could imagine.

Evening came and the man knocked on the barn door once again. "It's okay to come into the house now."

Tony and I left the cows and the safety of the barn and followed the farmer into his home. We were greeted by his wife and the wonderful aroma of paprika, meat, and roasted vegetables. The farmer's wife had a big pot of Hungarian Goulash bubbling on the stove for us. I don't think I've ever tasted better or eaten more.

"Let me show you how you get up to the attic where you will stay," the farmer said. "It's important you only come down when we tell you it's safe to do so and you will need to keep very quiet while you're up there."

"We will," I said.

"You are on your way to Austria, correct?"

Tony and I glanced at each other to confirm we both trusted these people before nodding in unison.

"We will figure out how we can help you."

"Thank you," I said, feeling myself choke up.

"We want you to succeed so you can have a better life in the West. We are tired of what life has become in Hungary, but we are old and want to die on Hungarian soil. Your lives are still ahead of you, and you need to live happily and free," the farmer said.

I was so overwhelmed I could only nod my appreciation.

"In order to do so, you must follow these ground rules: if some-one comes to see us, whether friend or foe, we will wake you up because we know when you are awake you will not make a noise. Don't light a light or smoke because the attic vent hole can be seen from the street."

"And I will bring you breakfast in the morning," his wife added.

"We'll discuss your next steps then," the farmer said directing us back up to the attic.

We did as we were told, both of us falling into a comfortable sleep that night, interrupted only by the sound of Russian soldiers chatting as they patrolled the village streets. When we awoke the next morning at dawn, it was a clear cold day. We remained completely silent.

"Good morning, gentlemen," the farmer's wife said, knocking on the attic door. "I brought you some breakfast."

It was a feast the likes of which we'd rarely seen since before the war—fresh bread, paprika bacon, homemade sausage, and fresh milk.

"I am going to check around the village and assess the situation," the farmer told us. "I will figure out the best way for you to proceed."

"Thank you so much. We truly appreciate your help," I said.

"And this wonderful food," Tony added.

"Just stay put until you hear from me," he said.

The burst of machine gunfire in the distance punctuated our need to stay put and remain quiet.

It was midafternoon when the farmer crept up to the attic. "The Austrian border is two kilometers to the west, and it is all farmland between here and there," he said. "I have learned there are observation towers every two hundred yards along the border with two soldiers in every tower— a machine gun operator and a searchlight operator. They scan the fields constantly, so the very best place to cross is between the two towers from 1:00 to 4:00 a.m. when the soldiers are most likely to be tired or asleep. When you see the searchlight coming towards you, hit the ground and don't move until it passes by. Needless to say, it's dangerous and you have to be very cautious. Don't be afraid to turn and come back here if it's too risky."

Heeding the farmer's further warning to avoid being seen in the village, we worked our way across moonlit fields. It wasn't long before we saw searchlights and heard the haunting rat-tat-tat of machine guns. As we inched closer to the border, the lights grew brighter, intermittently illuminating the area around us like a strobe.

As instructed, we threw ourselves to the ground and remained motionless whenever a roving spotlight approached. We assumed we were the only people out there, but while we were on the ground we could see more clearly and observed people to our left and right all attempting to do the same thing. The closer we got to the actual border, the more people we spotted around us.

Far too many.

We'd made it halfway, but decided it was just too risky and turned back.

Returning meant backtracking in the same manner as we had approached, diving to the ground, and staying completely still every time a light shone in our direction. We worked our way back slowly and made it back to the village safely. We returned to the farmhouse, but were even more careful this time, not entering the property from the street and making certain no one had seen us. We couldn't jeopardize the kindly people who'd taken us under their wing.

The farmer and his wife welcomed us back. Up we went to the attic once again to begin strategizing for our next attempt. Mid-afternoon the next day, the farmer said he'd heard about another method of escape. His uncle knew of a friend who'd collaborated with some Russian soldiers willing to take people safely to the border for $500 forints. All we had to do was meet up with a group of refugees at Ady Endre street at 8:00 p.m.

It sounded too easy, but we agreed to be at the designated spot at the given time. When we got there, we saw a group of at least thirty people eager to leave Hungary, some families with children. We were both suspicious given our previous experiences with the Russians and had a bad feeling about their plans to honor this particular business agreement. Instead of joining in, we hung back to see what transpired.

At 8:00 p.m. sharp, a truck pulled up driven by three Russian soldiers. One drove, the other remained in the passenger seat, and a third opened the back gate of the truck. He collected payment from the prospective passengers by way of cash, jewelry, and assorted valuables before allowing them to climb aboard. When the truck was full, the back gate was closed. The Russian with the gun shot a few rounds in the air.

The sound sent the two of us running in different directions.

An hour later, I was back at the farmer's house, but Tony was not. As it turned out, he ran to a house where some other kindly people took him in for the night. The next day, he found his way back to the last house in the village, where we had been waiting anxiously.

Later that day we learned we'd made another smart choice. The truck did not go to the Austrian-Hungarian border as promised. It was, as suspected, another setup by the Russians who turned all of the people into the authorities as escapees, and then kept their money, jewelry, and other valuables.

We spent one more day in the attic, preparing for another border-crossing attempt. While we had another day to enjoy kolbasz and pigs' cheese, fresh milk, and bread, the sound of Russian soldiers patrolling the village were a constant reminder of the danger we faced.

On November 29, 1956, darkness came, and we bid our goodbyes, once again thanking our kind hosts profusely for their wonderful food, help, and care.

"We will never forget you," I said.

The wife put her hands together and looked down, fighting tears. "Be careful."

Good luck, boys," the farmer said. "Remember, when the searchlight is coming toward you, lay down on the ground motionless."

With that, we gathered our two small handbags containing dry bread and bacon from home and the books I'd bought in the middle of the night in Székesfehérvár.

The lady of the house turned off all the lights so nobody could see us creep out the back gate. As we headed toward the railroad tracks,

I thought about what a shame it was we didn't know their names and they did not know ours. Really, it was better that way in case we got caught. With no names, we could not say who had helped us. I'm quite sure they felt the same way. We were just Hungarians to each other, which was all that mattered.

Once again, we found ourselves outside in the cold, crossing muddy farmland in pitch dark toward what we hoped was the border. We knew we'd come the right way when we spotted the flash of searchlights. As we began the harrowing process of repeatedly throwing ourselves to the ground, we spotted those attempting to escape all around us. A bit of additional advice the farmer had given me rang through my head, "Give it a little more time before you get up because if they see any movement, they will reverse the light to see what moved. You don't want to give them that advantage. It could cost you your life."

We realized there was a particular pattern the searchlight made as it maneuvered through the area. It was always the same, shifting only if the guards thought they detected movement. We decided it was best to crawl through that particular section. If we could get through the area quickly and in the dark, the next time the light strobed we would be safely ahead of the pattern.

We entered the danger zone along with about ten or twelve others, all of us hunkered down in the mud. It soon became apparent they were watching Tony and me for guidance. If we threw ourselves down on the ground, the group did the same.

"Don't move and don't speak," I told them, as we made our way past the tower.

When they could no longer reach us with their light, I assumed we'd crossed the border into Austrian territory. Our little group made it another 100 meters, when a boy of about twelve shouted, "We made it! We made it! We are in Austria!"

Terrified he'd given us up, at least eight of us jumped on him and pushed his head in the mud. We let him up for air when we realized no searchlight was coming and no bullets were hitting the ground around us.

We had made it!

Still, we were furious at the boy. After we let him up, we all lectured him sternly about how he'd endangered us and borders in Europe are not necessarily straight. We could have gone in the correct direction and unwittingly reentered Hungary.

We walked for nearly a kilometer in complete silence until we reached a small, paved road. Only then did we know for sure we were in Austria because the kilometer stones were different than the ones in Hungary. Relieved, but uncertain what was next, we kept going until we reached an area with a forest on one side and a vineyard on the other.

"I am an Austrian Border Patrol guard," said a voice in deeply accented Hungarian. "Are any of you carrying any weapons? If so, put them on the ground and stand back."

The voice came from behind a large oak tree.

"We are not going to shoot you," he continued. "We want to help. We are going to come down to the road and give you some instructions. And some chocolate."

When we confirmed we had no weapons, two Austrian border officers appeared from the forest in uniforms that definitely did not look like any Russian or any AVH uniforms we'd ever seen. They aimed strong flashlights on our vagabond refugee group. When they were convinced no one was carrying a gun, they approached.

"Welcomen zu Austria," one of them said, while the other gave us chocolates. "Keep walking on this road until you arrive at a small community about four kilometers from here. Somebody will be there to help you. If no one is there, find the little school on the side of this road. They'll give you food and information, and you can rest and sleep off the drama of your escape. Good luck to all of you."

With that, they disappeared back into the forest.

As daylight approached, we came upon something none of us had ever seen before—a very small, brand-new bus. It was empty, so we gathered around it and stared inside. Pretty soon an old man appeared from his field and greeted us in German.

"Gut Morgen. Schene little buus, yah?"

"Where is the motor?" I asked.

"Ah, yah," the old guy said. "Comen zi here."

We followed him to the back of this beautiful new VW bus. He opened the door and showed us the motor. We were all amazed by this marvel of German engineering.

We finally arrived at the Austrian village the border guard had told us about. We went over to the school and discovered it had been converted into a refugee hotel. I smelled Hungarian goulash and it made me a little nervous. Were we in Austria or had we been tricked back into Hungary? There were a lot of people around. Some spoke Austrian German and some of the locals were speaking Hungarian. That made me wonder because the Hungarian speakers looked like native Austrians and not like us. Their clothes were different.

"Why does everyone sound Hungarian but look Austrian?" I asked.

"Most of the people here are Hungarian or of Hungarian descent," one of the shelter workers told me. "This area of Austria was Hungarian territory until after the First World War and Trianon."

"What is Trianon?" I asked.

"One of the treaties that ended the First World War. It sanctioned the dismemberment of the Hungarian State."

Satisfied by her answer, I proceeded to stuff myself with goulash and palacsinta. Afterward, I was shown to a converted classroom to sleep off the drama of the past ten days. When I awoke, I was told I'd slept for almost two days. When I went to get dressed, I realized someone had cleaned, patched, and ironed my pants.

The simple act made me smile.

Refreshed, I walked around and surveyed the place. There were many new arrivals of every age, all of whom had enough of *Utopia* and had made the same perilous journey as Tony and me.

I decided to get something to eat and then walk around the village. Someone directed me through a small building situated on the road. From there, I could walk around and see the small community. I followed the directions, but another red bus blocked the entrance to the road. This bus was a lot like the VW bus, but four times in size. I went to examine this magnificent giant in its entirety. It was a Mercedes-Benz long-distance cruiser. It had curtains in each window. There were tables with little lamps between seats which faced each other. I assumed high-ranking government officials or even royalty traveled in this wonder.

I couldn't wait to see what was next in this incredible place and spent a glorious, peaceful day in the village enjoying its beauty and appreciating the semi-familiarity of Hungarian tradition in safe, free Austria.

The next morning there was an announcement to go to a certain room where we were to line up so they could get some identification information from each of us. They told us a bus would arrive by 1:00 p.m. We would be checked in by name and would then head to Traiskirchen refugee camp, which was very close to Vienna. The bus ride was to be free of charge, just as everything had been so far.

It almost felt too good to be true.

At 1:00 p.m., Tony and I gathered with the others as instructed. My name was called, and I stepped out the door of the building to the beautiful red Mercedes Benz bus. As Tony and I started up the steps, I couldn't believe the bus was for us! It smelled clean and fresh. There was carpet on the floor, and of course the little tables containing a lamp in front of each seat. Not to mention the bathroom at the back of the bus. I'd never been on anything so luxurious.

Once we were all accounted for and seated, the driver and an assistant came on board. "Guten Tag," they said with a smile. "We will have a great trip to Vienna."

With that, the big red beauty's diesel engine came to life. As everyone leaned back into the comfortable seats like aristocrats from old movies, it felt good to feel good, even if we had no idea what the future would bring. As Big Lizzy (as we'd taken to calling her) exited the narrow asphalt road and turned onto the four-lane concrete Austrian highway, we were all amazed by the smooth road and the clean, beautiful, manicured landscape. Hungary had been so ravaged, first by war, and then by the Communist regime there was no comparing what we now saw to what we'd left behind.

TRAISKIRCHEN

Tony and I waved "Aufviderzane" to the bus for the last time as we disembarked from Big Lizzy and were led to a large office area in the Traiskirchen complex.

The first step was an interview in which they collected data, identification, and information from all of us. The Austrian management showed us around the camp and explained the system governing the spotlessly maintained campus. Despite their quality management, one could still see the barbaric way it had been handled in the recent past.

Following the Second World War, Austria declared neutrality and the country was divided into four sectors: Russian, American, English, and French. Traiskirchen, an old army base that had been built before the First World War, was in the Russian sector. Austria was free of all Occupation forces by 1956, so the Russians were long gone but their names were carved everywhere on the walls, furniture, and woodwork.

The old army base was cleaned up but was not in use again until the Hungarian Revolution when the Russian forces reoccupied Hungary and refugees began to escape into Austria. There were multiple Hungarian refugee camps, but Traiskirchen became one of the largest in Austria.

After our orientation, we were divided into small groups and taken to the different rooms we would call home for the indefinite length of our stay. Tony and I were brought to a room with four bunk beds. There were only two open beds left in the room. Our other six roommates had been there for several weeks and were all from Budapest. While Tony and I were from Debrecen, we soon got to know them and became something of a family—albeit one borne out of our shared travails.

Sara and Josef wanted to emigrate to Brazil. Sandor was a photographer and wanted to emigrate to Venezuela. Eva was going to Canada. Károly, an architect, wanted to go to the USA, where Tony and I were heading. We all felt for Károly because he'd been at the camp the longest. He'd had several interviews with the U.S. Embassy in Vienna, but they had found a tiny black spot on his lungs. The spot was from a childhood sickness, and he was perfectly healthy, but it held up his paperwork indefinitely. Health requirements were very strict for the United States, so there was a long process ahead to get the medical clearance he needed.

There were about 5000 Hungarian refugees living on the campus at any given time. A lot of people wanted to stay in European countries—some because they had family in other places or did not want to venture too far from Hungary. Others, like Tony and me, were looking for a very different life.

Per the rules, we had to stay on campus unless we had a work permit or an Austrian took responsibility for us. Tony and I volunteered to work in a shop on campus to make beds for new arrivals. We also canvassed the old army base thinking about all the history that had happened there during the First World and Second World Wars, and now the refugee experience. I wondered what stories I would hear if the buildings could talk.

There were a number of Austrian university students who volunteered to work on campus in various administrative capacities, to help out as translators, and to take people into Vienna for various reasons. My favorite was a beautiful Austrian girl named Elizabeth.

Elizabeth and I became good friends. Apparently, she'd volunteered at the camp here and there, but once we started to chat, she came in almost every day. She got me passes to get out of the camp and would take me to tour Vienna. We went to museums, spent a day seeing the Schönbrunn Palace, and walked along the banks of the blue Danube—the same river that cut through Hungary. Interestingly enough, those walks always gave me slight homesickness, even while they helped me forget the danger I'd escaped from just six weeks earlier.

A week before Christmas, Elizabeth got Tony and I permits to go to Vienna. There was a streetcar train called the electric Bohnhoff. We got on with no ticket for the ride. The ticket person came by, but when he realized we were new refugees he allowed us to remain.

We couldn't believe he didn't throw us off the train; apparently, this kind of treatment was not the exception but the norm with the Austrians who were longtime partners with the Hungarians and very sympathetic to our plight.

We got off the streetcar in the middle of town. Snow was falling and everyone around us was carrying what we assumed were Christmas packages for their loved ones. We came to a large intersection where a policeman stood on a box directing traffic and saw he was surrounded by Christmas packages and decorated liquor bottles.

We realized the cars were stopping as they crossed the intersection and leaving packages and gifts for him. After a while, the packages accumulated to such a degree a police car showed up and loaded up the packages to ease traffic. Later, we were told that happened all over the city at Christmas time.

We were awed by the beauty of this tradition.

My friend Elizabeth told me the day before Christmas there was to be a big surprise: A very important American was coming to the campus to make a speech to us, the Hungarian refugees.

On Christmas Eve, at least 2000 of us filled the big hall. We were not only surprised but overwhelmed when Vice President Richard Nixon stepped up to the microphone and began to speak. A translator repeated his words in Hungarian. There wasn't a single one of us who expected such an important person in our midst.

When the vice president finished his speech, the curtain opened stage right and a number of people appeared and began to hand each other red and green nylon bags until they ended up with Nixon. He then motioned the people in the first row to come to the stage where he shook each person's hand and presented each of them with a gift. In fact, everyone in the auditorium got a Christmas package from the Vice President of the United States of America including Tony and me. Inside the bag were gifts for men, women, and children. I found a bottle of shaving cream in mine and didn't know what it was because it was an American brand. There was also Colgate toothpaste and a toothbrush, Hershey chocolate bars, Dove soap, note pads, and ballpoint pens.

We simply couldn't believe the number two man in America had come thousands of miles bearing Christmas gifts for us, a ragtag band of refugees from behind the Iron Curtain.

America was called *heaven* in Hungary. We now knew why.

One morning, as we were making the rounds on the grounds of the base, we heard a commotion between two of the older buildings. There was screaming and yelling in Hungarian. A man was on the ground being kicked and bitten by several other refugees.

"What's going on?" we asked, running over. "What did he do?"

"That man is a spy!" someone shouted. "He is collecting information and has close to a thousand names. He is a Communist dog working for the Russians in Hungary. We have to watch these dirty bastards. They take this information back to Hungary and use it against our family and friends. A couple weeks ago they caught another one who'd even taken photos."

We watched as the Austrian campus police took the man away from the angry attackers before it was too late.

One day, Elizabeth said, "I'm going to take you to Vienna to introduce you to my parents. I told my mother about you, and she would like it if we stopped by."

"Of course," I said.

She had a car, so we drove to her house. It was actually more of a villa and was located in the most desirable part of Vienna. Her home was surrounded by other big homes and parks, the likes of which I had never seen before.

All of a sudden, I started to worry. "Look at me," I said. "I am in the same clothes I escaped with from Hungary. I have a patch on my left knee. What will your mother say when she sees me?"

"Don't worry," she said. "She wanted to meet you because I told her a lot of nice things about you."

As we walked up to the front door. I spotted her mother checking us out through the window. Then, I stepped inside the most opulent home I had ever seen. There was gold, silver, and expensive porcelain everywhere; I couldn't have felt more awestruck.

"What does your father do for a living?" I asked.

"He is in the sugar manufacturing industry," she said.

Elizabeth introduced me to her mother, "This is János, a friend from the refugee camp where I help out."

Elizabeth and I understood each other easily with a mixture of German, English, and Hungarian words. We really had very little problem communicating. The same wasn't quite as true when trying to speak with her mother, whose disapproval was evident in her pinched smile. It was clear she wasn't interested in getting to know a penniless refugee, no matter how much her only daughter might like him. I was simply a momentary distraction. Nothing more.

It would have hurt, except I knew she was right. I cared for Elizabeth, but our futures were destined to be very different.

While I continued to enjoy spending time with Elizabeth, Tony grew close with an attractive female refugee. We became somewhat independent of each other but were still good friends. One day, we got a letter addressed to both of us from the people who ran the bed shop where we worked. Inside was a thank you for our hard work, a bit of compensation, and two tickets to a famous operetta at the well-known Burg Theater.

As an aspiring actor, I was beyond excited. To top it all off, the star of this production was a beautiful Hungarian named Marika Rökk who had fled the country at the beginning of the Second World War and become a major star in Vienna. I couldn't believe I was going to get to see her perform with top billing in the middle of Vienna.

The day came. We cleaned up best we could, but we were still wearing the patched-up pants and clothing we had escaped in. We called it the *Refugee Uniform*. Looking as good as we could, we got on the electric Bohnhoff to Vienna from Traiskirchen and arrived at the beautiful, grand, old Burg Theater.

A nice older employee came up to us, looked at our tickets, and waved her flashlight so we would follow her. We went into the dark theater just as the curtain was about to rise. She led us all the way down to the third-row center and stopped. I thought for sure she'd made some mistake. She checked our tickets and nodded in confirmation.

Amazed by our incredible seats, we shuffled into the center of the row, careful not to step on anyone's toes. The moment we sat down, the curtain came up and the show began. When Marika Rökk took center stage, she received thunderous claps. Some people even stood. We couldn't have enjoyed the first half of the performance more.

When the lights went up for intermission, we looked up and admired the grand crystal chandelier, waiting for most everyone else to file out while we worked up the courage to follow the crowd. We only had enough to buy a cigarette each, nothing else. People looked at us strangely, no doubt because of our shabby, patched clothing. We felt so self-conscious amongst these well-dressed people we hid in a corner behind a large pillar to smoke where we wouldn't be seen. I watched two couples a few yards away. The men were in tuxedos. The ladies wore long evening dresses, jewelry, and had furs draped over their shoulders. They were all drinking champagne. One of the ladies kept looking in our direction and then back at her companions.

One of the men left the group and disappeared into the crowd. He returned a few minutes later with sandwiches on a silver tray and two glasses of champagne. One of the ladies took the tray and headed in our direction. The other lady joined her. When they reached us, they smiled, said something in German, handed us the tray, and walked away.

I almost dropped the tray because my cigarette was burning my hand.

After I regained my composure, I felt angry. *We're not beggars. We don't need other people's pity,* I thought looking at the sandwiches and the champagne. As I looked back at the two couples, they smiled and lifted their glassed to greet us. I realized they had made this gesture out of sympathy and support. They saw how we were dressed and knew we were not beggars, but escapees from *Utopia* who had risked our lives in our quest for freedom.

When it was time to go back to our seats along with the rest of the opulent crowd, I said *danke schoen* to them. They smiled generously in return.

The joy I felt for the theater had never been so intense.

We had a similar experience when we went for our fourth interview at the American Embassy. It was 11:00 a.m. and we were walking by a restaurant, once again wearing our refugee uniform.

"Comen zi hear, bite," said the person standing in the doorway. "Come in my friends," he said again, and bid us to come inside the restaurant, where he led us to a table.

We did not know what to expect.

A few minutes went by, and two beers appeared on our table. The waiter said, "Drink, drink, bruder."

"We don't have any schillings," I said.

"Drink, drink," he said again. "It's okay."

We were halfway done when the waiter brought out two of the biggest wiener schnitzels I'd ever seen. They were so big they were hanging off the oval plate. We looked at him in total disbelief. "No schilling. We can't pay," I said again.

"Enjoy," he said. "No charge."

We ate, our hearts once again full of appreciation. They knew we could never afford it, make it, or pay for it, and wanted us to enjoy the bounty of their great cooking.

The experience kept us feeling warm and confident during our wait on line in front of the American embassy. It was a cold blustery day and everyone else shivered in hats, gloves, and warm clothes.

Tony and I felt invincible as we discussed our future in America. We decided we were somehow going to learn to drive and then acquire a truck and haul freight across America. That way we would make a living and also get to see our new, wonderous country. We spoke of New York, The White House, Gettysburg, the Grand Canyon, and Sierra Nevada from the Westerns we'd read growing up. Of course, we also wanted to go to California where all the gold was, and figured we'd maybe even get pickaxes and become gold miners.

The line moved slowly as we fantasized about our future.

"How much do you think a used truck will cost in Detroit?" Tony asked.

"They must be cheaper there than anywhere else because that's where American cars are made."

"Where will we get the money for it?"

"We'll figure that out when the time comes."

Two men approached the line wearing only shirts and thin pants.

"They are going to freeze in this weather," I said.

As they began to walk by, I recognized one of them as Lendvay Lajos, Europe's most famous cinder motorbike racer. He was from Debrecen, and I'd passed his family's motorbike-repair shop every day on my way to school. I had not only seen him there but spoken with him several times. He was famous in Hungary, and Europe as well. At one point, he'd won a big cinder race in Czechoslovakia and the prize was money and a beautiful red sports car with a canvas top. It was a very big deal, especially in a place where you were not allowed to own a car or anything considered to be a capitalistic endeavor.

"Tony that's Lendvay," I said as he passed by us.

The man heard me say his name and stopped. "Hey, are you guys from Debrecen?"

"Yes, we are," I said. "What are you doing in just a thin shirt in this weather?"

"We sold our coats to some refugees for food," he said, clearly having been through some of the same trials and tribulations as the rest of us.

"Aren't you cold?" I asked beginning to take off my coat to give him my sweater.

"No, no, it's okay. We are used to it now."

"How long have you been in Austria?" Tony asked.

"We escaped from Hungary and proceeded through Austria without checking in with the Austrian authorities before crossing into Germany."

"You didn't check in at all?"

"We figured we'd go straight to our German racing buddies. I am sure they would have helped and sponsored us except the German border patrol turned us away. They said we had to register with the Austrian government and then apply to come to Germany if that's what we wanted to do."

"So, you guys escaped through two countries?"

"Yes," Lendvay said.

"What now?" I asked.

"We are headed to register with the Austrian authorities to become Hungarian Refugees in Austria. The office is this way," he said pointing not too far past the end of our line.

"Then you'll go to Germany to your cinder racing buddies?"

"Yes. We'll try."

"And you'll race for Germany?"

"We'll see," Lendvay said, and they waved goodbye.

I knew he wouldn't have any problems given he was known all over Europe.

"At least they didn't get shot," I said to Tony. "But the law is the law."

Years later, I heard Lendvay ended up in England where he raced for a while and then went into business there. I always wondered what had happened to the pretty red Skoda sports car he'd won back in the day.

At the U.S. Embassy, Tony and I were taken to different offices and interviewed separately. This was my fourth interview with the same interviewer. He already knew everything about me—my family, where I'd gone to school, where we lived, and a lot more. How he'd acquired that information I wasn't sure because I did not tell him. I was quite sure the Hungarian government was not cooperating with the American Embassy, so I wondered but didn't dare ask. I felt at ease with him, though. He was about thirty years old and spoke perfect Hungarian. This time, I worked up the courage to ask him if he was of Hungarian descent.

"No," he said. "I am an American. When I enlisted in the Foreign Service, one of the languages I chose to learn was Hungarian."

"I've been told it's a hard one," I said.

"It's a phonetic language, so you say the words as they are written, but the grammar is a killer."

This fourth meeting was about thirty minutes and more of a friendly conversation than anything else.

"Okay," he said as we were wrapping up. "We'll inform you through the Traiskirchen office about what comes next. Thank you and good luck to you."

"Thank you," I said as he reached out to shake my hand.

I left the meeting uncertain whether his sendoff had been a positive or a negative sign. Would I be allowed to go to America or not? Unlike me, Tony was not worried. After all, his entry to the U.S. was set because he had an aunt and uncle who were United States citizens. I had no one there to sponsor me.

"Don't worry," Tony told me as we started back toward the camp. "They will sponsor you as well."

I tried to hold his words in my heart.

GOOD NEWS

There was a building on the Traiskirchen compound where representatives from Western European companies and factories could set up shop for a few days at a time to interview refugees who wanted to go to a particular country to live and work. If the company was interested in them, they would be sponsored to move to the country of their choice. These recruiting agents traveled to the various refugee camps to find refugees to come to their countries. Tradespeople and doctors were in especially high demand.

Tony and I were determined to go to the United States, but knowing these agents went to all the refugee camps in Austria, I would stop in at the temporary recruiting offices to ask if I could look at some of the names they signed up in the hopes of finding friends, relatives, or anyone else I might recognize.

One day, there were two agents on campus from Great Britain. They had no customers in their office that morning and seemed happy for me to walk in.

Good morning," I said in English.

"You speak English," one of them said enthusiastically.

"Good morning, good day, I love you, and hands up!" I said, giving them my whole repertoire.

They both laughed.

I'd learned to bridge the language gap by speaking with my hands and using body language. It took some doing, but I managed to make the men understand I wasn't looking to move to England myself but wanted to see the list of people from other refugee camps who had signed up to live and work there.

They had come from Wollsdorf the day before and allowed me to see the names of the people they'd registered. As I was scanning the list, one name jumped out from the middle of the page:

Istvan Czingula.

"Oh my god! My brother!" I said aloud. Despite my mother's wishes, my brother Istvan had safely escaped from Hungary. "Wollsdorf, right?"

"Yes, Wollsdorf," the British agent said.

I shouted with joy.

I needed to get to Wollsdorf. I don't know how far it was, or how I would get there, but I was going ASAP. I sprinted over to the building where Elizabeth worked. She would know what to do to help me get there.

"She's not due in until noon," one of her colleagues said.

I waited impatiently until she showed up.

"My brother Istvan is at the Wollsdorf refugee camp!" I said, speaking fast in my rudimentary German with way too much excitement.

Although she'd taught me a lot, there was no way anyone could possibly translate what I was trying to say accurately. She understood enough to smile as she went to find someone who spoke fluent Hungarian.

As soon as she had the full story and could make the arrangements, we were in her car on our way to Wollsdorf!

We arrived at a much smaller camp with far fewer amenities than we had in Traiskirchen. We charged into the camp manager's office, and I began to explain why we were there. Thankfully, Elizabeth took over in German. After a moment or two, the manager went over to his desk and began to leaf through his files.

"Ine moment bite?" he asked in German.

"Istvan Czingula," I said.

"Stephan," she said, translating his name into German.

The manager flipped a couple pages, smiled happily, and said, "Aha, Istvan!"

He proceeded to speak to Elizabeth in German.

I watched her face drop.

"Yes, he was here," she finally said, "but he signed up to go to England and left last night."

While I would have preferred to see my brother in the flesh, I knew he had made it out of Hungary safely. "That's good news because I know he is okay," I said, hugely relieved to know he was unharmed. "Where did he sign up to work?"

"The British National Coal Board," she said.

My brother, who had been studying to be a cabinet maker, was now going to the U.K. to become a coal miner. Our destinies were nothing if not ever-changing. I would learn later Istvan and a friend took off a week after my departure. It turned out he'd been looking for me in Austria through the Red Cross, but they could not locate me. He went to be a coal miner because they offered him very good pay, which was something he could never make in Hungary. He took the offer along with his friend.

I'd missed him by one day, but I was happy as we drove back to Traiskirchen, because I left with his address.

I wrote to him right away.

Over the next few days, Elizabeth and I took in some more of beautiful Vienna. One day, after another excursion to the exquisite Schönbrunn Palace, I went back to my room on campus and was handed a letter by one of my roommates.

I looked at the return address and about fainted: the American Embassy of Vienna.

Tony had already opened his and had a huge grin on his face. My roommates all clamored for me to open mine.

My hand shook as I opened the envelope.

I was accepted into the United States of America!

"I told you!" Tony said as we hugged gleefully.

Along with the welcome letter were instructions. First, we were to be transferred to Salzburg where we would receive further instructions.

Everyone was happy for us, even Károly, who'd already spent two and half months trying to get cleared to go to the United States. We knew we were all to spread out across the globe and would possibly never see each other again, but each of us had something better on the horizon.

Suddenly, I thought about Elizabeth. How was she going to react to my news? Surely, she'd seen other Hungarian immigrants come and go, but I knew her expectations about me were somewhat different. She knew I would leave for the United States, but I don't think she expected it to happen so soon.

We met up on campus the next day.

"I have been accepted into America," I told her.

"That's great news," she said, genuinely happy for me.

And then I told her the time frame. "I leave tomorrow."

"Tomorrow?" she said, her voice raising an octave.

"We are being transferred to Salzburg in the morning."

Tears gathered in her eyes. "Salzburg is beautiful! I will come visit you there. There is a castle on top of a hill overlooking the city. You will love it."

As we cried and held each other, I didn't have the heart to tell her I'd probably only be there five days.

The next morning, Tony and I went to meet the bus bound for Salzburg. Elizabeth was not there, which made it easier because I already missed her.

A big Mercedes bus full of future Americans pulled out of Traiskirchen refugee camp. The ride was comfortable and the landscape magnificent: clean, well-kept villages, cities, and farmland dotted by new farmhouses. A lady came along as our caretaker, distributing sandwiches at noon, and tea and coffee along the way. It was such a stark difference from where we'd been a few months earlier, but the enormity of it all hit me and I couldn't help but feel a little homesick.

The bus pulled into Salzburg, but did not stop in the city proper. Instead, we were taken to an ex-American army base. This was the last place we would stay before we departed for the USA. We did not know exactly when or whether we would be placed onto an airplane or a ship, but we knew we would find out in a few days.

Tony and I were directed to a modern, large room with thirty or forty foldable steel beds. To the right of my bed was an older lady. She was heading to join her brother who'd left Hungary for America before the Russians invaded. We were all given a package with necessities like toothpaste, toothbrush, soap, etc. Everyone also received a World War II American Army jacket.

I had a nice dinner in the cafeteria and went to bed about 9:30 p.m. The next morning, Tony and I got permission to go into historic Salzburg, a magnificent city of grand old buildings and churches, pruned trees, and spotless sidewalks.

The castle on the hill that Elizabeth had mentioned beckoned in the distance. I could not leave Salzburg without visiting the castle and learning its history. We were told we had a few days left on the base, so we planned more visits into the city and, of course, a tour of Salzburg Castle.

The next morning, Tony and I got up at 4:00 a.m. and went into town. We expected the city to be sleeping. Instead, there were homeowners all around sweeping and hosing down the sidewalks in front of their buildings. By the time the sun came up, the city was bright and clean.

As we started up the hill toward the castle, I thought about Elizabeth and how she'd wanted to take me here. I missed her and thought about how privileged I'd been to know her, but America pulled at my heart.

Three years old in Hatvan, 1940

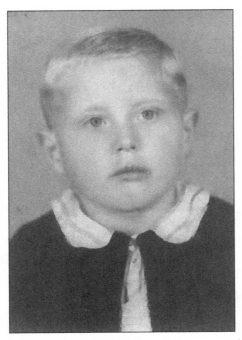

My brother, Istvan Czingula in Debrecen, 1944

Family photo

With my high school buddies at Lake Balaton, 1953

My high school graduation photo

The Gang of Árpád Square

Toni and my roommates at Traiskirchen

With Toni and some friends at Traiskirchen

View from the train to Bremerhaven

US Army Transportation Ship, The General Nelson M. Walker

The view from the General Walker

On the boat with the Merchant Marines

In Detroit, Michigan, USA with Toni beside his cousin's new Oldsmobile

Main Street, Crawfordsville, Indiana

With Olivia and friends at Wabash College

Painting the Phi Delta Theta house

Visiting the Empire State Building

Reunited with Istvan (Steven) in Beverly Hills

At Venice Beach with my first car, a 1940 Oldsmobile

My mom, sisters, and niece

My first professional photo shoot

At the Elm Drive apartment

Wearing the one shirt I brought from Hungary

Looking like James Dean

Headshot

Reuniting with our mother at LAX in 1965

My true love, the Jaguar

Demonstrating my very first invention

Ribbon cutting at one of my many business ventures, the Quik Car Wash

The original Detroit West Body Shop on Pico Boulevard

With Rose Mary Welch and John Perkins Barrymore at my production of "An Evening with John Barrymore."

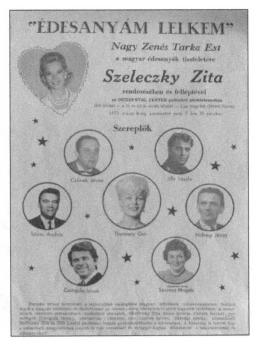

Hungarian play along with well-known performers
including Thuróczy Gizi and Szeleczky Zita

Modeling for J.C. Penney, 1971

With my father on his first visit to the United States

With actress Miko Taka and the winner of the Long Beach Beauty Contest

With Cesar Romero and company at the Motion Picture Country Home

With my friend, Mrs. Frances X. Bushman and
Mary Francis Montague a well-known model

Headshot

With my beautiful son

Christian in front of his trailer on set

Christian and Lauritz Melchior's son at the AIFA luncheon

Plans for The Atrium in Whittier, California

With SPI board of directors member Art Linkletter

Groundbreaking ceremony for Nevada Solar One

With my beautiful twin granddaughters Lili and Eden

Siblings reunited

BREMERHAVEN

We got word one night we were to be up and ready by 4:00 a.m. the next morning for a bus ride to the railroad station. We'd be going through Germany by train to the port city of Bremerhaven.

We were going to cross the Atlantic Ocean by boat.

I woke up in the morning before dawn and gathered my belongings. My American army jacket was on the end of my bed, not where I usually put it. I started to put my arm into my sleeve and noticed, to my amazement, the Hungarian emblem used in the revolution of 1956 had been embroidered over the heart.

For a second, I wondered what was going on. Then, I saw the lady whose bed was next to mine was smiling. There were also tears collecting in the corners of her eyes. I teared up as well when I realized she'd embroidered that all-important symbol onto my most prized possession.

I went around to her bed and hugged her for a long time. As I held her, she whispered. "I stitched the emblem for you to always remember where you are from and who you are, no matter where your destiny takes you. God bless you and good luck to you!"

At that moment, I thought of her as the mother of all Hunnia. I thought about Attila the Hun who brought his Nomadic tribe to the

Carpathian Basin. Then, I recalled Saint Steven, the first Christian King of Hungary, crowned by the Pope more than a 1000 years earlier. I thought of King Matyas, and then of Kossuth Lajos, who was the president of Hungary in 1848. I even thought about the First World War when we lost two-thirds of the territory known as Hungary. I had been a child survivor of the Second World War and thoughts of the Germans and Russians filled my brain. I thought of all the history and tragedies of our people in just a few seconds.

I just stood there in silence, holding my American jacket with the Hungarian emblem until I heard Tony yell, "Come on, it's time to go."

Ten Mercedes-Benz buses lined up at the refugee camp. Officials checked everyone's American Embassy papers. There were hundreds and hundreds of us from various buildings and I thought, *My God, is there anyone left in Hungary?*

The busses drove in a caravan to the train station, emptied out, and we were led into specially reserved railroad cars. As the train filled and we started moving, Tony and I looked back at the beautiful city, which was home to Mozart and the castle on the hill.

"Let's come back for a visit someday when we have money," I said to Tony.

"Oh yes," he said. "Definitely."

Most of us had never even heard of Bremerhaven. In the Communist school system, we were not taught European or Western History at all. Europe, and the West in general, were considered *Enemies of the People*. There was no geography, history, or Western language taught in Hungarian Schools, only Russian, which was compulsory. When we reached the German border, three officers came on board and checked the list provided by our Austrian handlers and managers. They proceeded through the entire train to check paperwork for each of us. The process took less than an hour. Suddenly, we were rolling again, now through Germany. We saw villages, cities, and farms along the way. The famed Autobahn paralleled the train and I marveled at all the German-made cars, busses, and motorcycles that whizzed by. That was the day I learned there was no speed limit.

At noon, the train slowed, and we approached a station in one of the larger cities. We heard music and saw a lot of people congregating on the platform. As it turned out, they had all gathered to greet us. When the train stopped, we weren't allowed to get off, but were treated to well-wishers waving German and Hungarian flags. Some handed us little packages, sandwiches, and even beer!

"Why is there so much enthusiasm for our train and its passengers?" I asked one of the older passengers who spoke German.

"They admire that a small country was able to chase out the mighty Soviet Occupational Army from Hungarian territory, even temporarily. East Germany is still under Soviet rule and many Germans have suffered."

I felt both heartened and sad. A lot of people had died for those five days of freedom. Why was I so lucky to be able to take in the lovely German countryside and its appreciative residents on the way to total freedom in America?

After half an hour, we waved goodbye and started moving again. We now had a new steam engine pulling us towards Bremerhaven, or so we were told by the German managers who'd joined the Austrians for the remainder of our train ride.

We arrived in Bremerhaven on February 5, 1957, and were transported to a harbor filled with huge oceangoing ships. We all made bets as to which ship would be ours. Hundreds of Hungarian refugees crowded the harbor building. A temporary office was set up with several desks. We were asked to line up in front of the desks and check in. Once we were cleared, we were led to another section of the depot building. When a group of about fifty people had collected, we were walked out of the building, onto the dock, and led toward a huge, gray oceangoing ship with *General Walker* emblazoned on it.

The American flag flew from the side.

From the dock, it looked several stories high. We got to a gangplank and followed our agent aboard one by one. He handed each of us a printed piece of paper that stated, *The General Walker is a United States Navy transportation ship. This ship was used in World War II to transport United States Marines and Army personnel to liberate people from the Nazis. The United States Government provided this ship for your transportation to the United States. The ship's personnel are all merchant marines; however, the captain is a United States Naval Officer. When everyone is on board and the ship is on its way, the captain will address the passengers.*

I felt proud to be on an American ship being liberated from Communism with 2,000 of my fellow countrymen, all of whom were hoping for a better life and future in America. I thought about Columbus and his three wooden ships, which took three months to arrive in the New World. I calculated this steel behemoth would get us there in less than a third of that time. I looked forward to every moment of the journey with the enthusiasm of a boy who'd always been fascinated by different modes of transportation, and a young man who'd fled everything he knew for a life of freedom.

We were led to a large area of the ship and were startled to see rows of beds hanging from the walls four bunks high. I quickly assessed the situation and claimed the lowest canvas bed by throwing my small bag onto it.

Tony followed my example. We both guarded our chosen berths by sitting on them, which was a production until we got the hang of it. We thought we had everything figured out to our advantage until somebody claimed the hanging bed above me. When that person climbed onto his bed, it sank down nearly to my face. This sleeping arrangement would prove strange to adjust to, but at least I did not have to climb up to the fourth berth to go to sleep.

Once our bunk arrangements were secured, we went up to the top deck—the equivalent of climbing up the stairs of a five-story building. We wanted to see and experience the harbor and watch the loading of our ship. We reached the top deck and heard music below from the dock. Sure enough, there was yet another German brass band, this one all in short leather pants, playing traditional German folk tunes for our send-off to the new world.

LADY LIBERTY

We set sail from Bremerhaven. On the first leg of the journey, *the General Walker* anchored in the English Channel very close to the White Cliffs of Dover, a place I never thought I see. While I was awed by sheer, chalk white cliffs jutting up beside the sea, I couldn't help but feel a bit nervous. Most of us did. Why had the ship stopped? Was the ship going to turn around and take us back?

When a small boat approached and uniformed English personnel boarded via special equipment, we tried not to panic. We held our breath while they attended to some sort of official business, none of which involved anything to do with us immigrants at all. We breathed a collective sigh of relief when they departed two hours later, and we were on our way to New York.

The first five days of sailing went smoothly. Tony and I explored the ship and made some friends among the merchant marines. They gave us cigarettes—not just one or two, but a whole pack. My favorite brand was Pall Mall.

Seagulls, lots of them, landed on deck all night long looking for food scraps and proceeded to dive on the garbage that was thrown into the ocean.

The food was good, but very different. The first time I ever had a banana, it was on the *General Walker*. Where was the paprika? Tony and I vowed to teach America to cook the Hungarian way once we got to the U.S.

The day always started with endless medical examinations by multiple doctor/examiners looking for different sicknesses, existing or new. They would take fifteen people at a time to the belly of the ship, three or four stories below the waterline. We were lined up, and one or two doctors searched for signs of whatever disease was on the day's agenda. One morning, I was lined up with fifteen or so other men. The female doctor signaled everyone to open their belt and let their pants down. We did what we were told, but that was not enough. She motioned everyone to drop their underpants. Some of the men pretended not to understand her command, so she went down the line and motioned for everyone to push their undergarments down to their feet. It was clear she was an army doctor and had done this drill before.

With all eyes on the ceiling, she and an assistant started at the top of the line. The assistant took notes while she examined everyone in a very personal way.

Thank God she wore rubber gloves.

On the fifth day, the weather grew rough and didn't let up. It is not advisable for today's ocean liners to cross the Atlantic in February. In our old navy ship, the fifteen-to-twenty-foot waves tossed us around relentlessly. Almost everyone got seasick. Tony and I became dizzy, but neither of us were throwing up nonstop like so many of our fellow passengers. When the merchant marines saw we were okay, they gave us bags to hand out to those who needed them or were about to.

The captain got on the speakers and warned us to be careful, the waves were likely to get even bigger. The doors leading to the open deck were closed to avoid anyone being swept out to sea. The bow of the ship would rise, a wave would roll beneath us and lift the transom so the back would rise making the front of the ship go under the next wave until the entire front half was under water. This happened over and over for days. The crew began putting diesel fluid in the water system so people would not drink it. Too much liquid in the stomach caused people to get sick sooner.

By the eighth day the sea began to level off. The waves became smaller, and travel became bearable once again. Those of us who'd managed with the least amount of sea sickness had to help with the massive cleanup of the ship's interior. No cabin remained untouched, and the hallways bore the brunt of people getting sick for days on end.

On the second to last day of our journey, the ship suddenly slowed. It was rumored we'd be arriving in New York the next day and they had slowed down to give everyone time to recover from the ravages of seasickness, get a good night's sleep, and be healthy for our arrival in New York Harbor.

We all went to sleep with dreams of our new life in our heads.

I woke up on February 14, 1957, to cries of "We are there! We are there!"

Two thousand people ran simultaneously to the upper deck to a beautiful calm day, just as the sun was about to rise.

How lucky we all are, I thought.

I heard yells of "Look over there," and saw some people point to something in the distance protruding from the water.

"What is it?" people asked one another as the mysterious object grew in height, rising—or so it appeared—straight out of the sea.

"It looks like a torch!"

"There's an arm holding the torch!"

The arm became more and more visible as the ship progressed slowly forward. A head with a crown on it appeared, seemingly, from just below the surface of the water.

As we approached, the body of the statue rose to greet us with the sun shining upon it.

The Statue of Liberty is a marvel to behold under any circumstance. For me and my fellow two thousand passengers, all of whom had survived the horrors of war, the tyranny of Communism, and risked death and an uncertain future in the hopes of a better life, there is no way to fully describe how incredible a sight Lady Liberty truly was on that brilliant morning.

We were all so incredibly overcome with emotion, the entire ship broke into a spontaneous version of the Hungarian national anthem, tears streaming down our faces. We didn't know our new anthem yet, but realized we'd soon be learning the words to an equally important song.

We learned the captain had planned this extraordinary finale to our excursion. Despite everyone's desire to get there in a hurry, he'd slowed down the ship for the last ten hours, adjusting the speed so two thousand Hungarian refugees who'd lost their homeland would behold the unforgettable sight of the Statue of Liberty in the dawn's early light.

People continued to stare at Lady Liberty even after the ship had passed by and was replaced by the equally awe-inspiring New York skyline. Our ship moved ever more slowly through the port traffic. Tugboats appeared and started to push, pull, and shove the *General Walker* into its berth.

When all the giant ropes and anchors were in place to the satisfaction of the captain, the order of disembarkation was announced. There was only one way to exit the heroic ship—single file, just like it had been done during the Second World War. We all had to go to a certain deck from where the disembarkation plank was secured. It was a narrow plank that went down in a 45-degree slope to the terminal floor. It was a long, slow, nerve-wracking descent, but the moment we stepped off the ramp and onto the terminal floor, we were, for the first time in our lives, on United States terra firma.

Civilian officials then directed us to a line of tables, behind which, a person smiled and welcomed us to the United States.

As I got close to stepping down off the platform, I noticed there was an unarmed American soldier in uniform. He was trying to get someone's attention, but none of the new immigrants would engage with him. When I got closer, I decided I would speak to him, or at least, shake his hand. The soldier told me in broken Hungarian he had volunteered to go to Hungary and free the Hungarian people from Russian Occupation.

"Tens of thousands of us volunteered, but the U.S. government would not let us go," the soldier said. As someone behind me tried to translate, I was pushed forward in line. He could not follow me because there was a system of official registration. The soldier went back to the end of the platform to find another person who would listen to his touching story.

A kind lady asked me in Hungarian for my various identification papers.

"Are you Hungarian?" I asked her.

"I am an American," she said.

"How come you speak such good Hungarian?"

"I learned when I signed up for the Foreign Service," she said. "And you will learn English in no time."

"I hope so," I said.

"Do you know any English words?"

I repeated my repertoire: "I Love you. Yes. No. Hands up!"

She laughed and said, "Welcome to America!"

I was shown into the terminal along with nearly forty others. *Now what?* I wondered.

A bus appeared with United States Army written on the side.

"Hey, wait for me!" I heard Tony say from behind me.

We boarded together, headed toward New Jersey and a place called Camp Kilmer where we would begin our new life as Americans.

DETROIT

Camp Kilmer was a large army base where the American soldiers were collected before they were sent off to fight in World War II. Still a working base, a section was set aside for Hungarian refugees. Tony and I spent ten days there and made our first two dollars by helping peel potatoes in the kitchen. We spent our earnings at the PX on a box of Hershey bars, which we ate until we were sick.

At the end of our stay, Tony and I were taken to the railroad station where we settled in for the trip to Detroit. He would remain with his relatives permanently. I was invited to live with them until I figured out what was next for me. I was nervous about my fate, since I was not related and had no idea how I would be received by the relatives of a friend, but I reveled in all the new sights and sounds as the train made its way across the Northeast and into the Rust Belt.

My fears disappeared when we arrived, and Tony's aunt and uncle greeted both of us with open arms. Tony's aunt looked like his mother's twin, so she felt like a familiar face. His uncle, a short much older man with thick glasses, was warm and kind.

It was snowy, cold, and icy as we walked to a parking lot full of cars—more than we'd ever seen in one place. We stopped at a shiny new yellow passenger car. Tony and I looked at each other and he whispered to me, "It's a Chrysler!"

We climbed into the back seat, and looked over his uncle's shoulder, fascinated by how this vehicle worked. There were no visible gear shift and only two pedals on the floor. We couldn't believe it when his uncle moved a handle on the dashboard and began to back out of the parking space. No gear changed, and it seemed as though there was no clutch at all. We had never seen anything like that, but I was too nervous to ask any questions.

I didn't dare imagine what their home would actually look like and was delighted when we arrived at 7551 Osage Street, the address we both knew by heart. It was an attractive, two story home on a tidy residential street. We were amazed to discover there was also a third level—a completely built-out basement!

We met Tony's cousin Lajos (Luis, as he was known in the United States). He was nineteen. We also met Cousin Ida who was thirty-five years old. We were then shown to the bedroom we would share for the duration of my stay. Excited but thoroughly exhausted, we both went right to sleep. The next morning, we piled into the big new Chrysler and were taken to a men's clothing store where Tony's generous relatives bought us American-style suits, shirts, and shoes.

We had truly arrived!

On March 23, 1957, I celebrated my 20th birthday in Detroit, Michigan, USA.

"Go into town," Tony's uncle said. "Enjoy yourself."

I asked Tony to come along with me.

"Go on by yourself and don't feel any need to hurry back," his aunt said. "I need Tony to help me with something."

I hadn't told anyone it was my birthday, but I wished I'd felt a little more welcome, just the same. Feeling as though they wanted to get rid of me for the day so they could have family time, I sauntered off alone, feeling a little sorry for myself.

I milled around downtown, looking into shop windows, and seeing what there was to see. I chanced by a movie house. In those days, you could see three new movies for fifty cents. I had nothing to do, and knew no one wanted me hanging around the house, so I figured I'd just stay for all three shows.

Even though I couldn't understand much of the dialogue, one of the movies, *Oklahoma*, cheered me up. I was in America and, someday, I too would be on the big screen.

It was dark when the last movie ended. So was the house when I returned. The only light was in the basement, so I tiptoed downstairs quietly to avoid waking anyone. In the basement rec room, I discovered balloons and a big table covered in half-eaten food and cake. I assumed that was why they had wanted me out of the house—a party where I wasn't invited. At least I hadn't come home in the middle of whatever it was they were celebrating.

The next morning, I learned it was supposed to be a surprise party for me!

I was so new in the country, I didn't understand any of the subtleties going on and they didn't provide me enough clues, much less a time to return so I would. It was an embarrassing misunderstanding, and I was left feeling bad, and touched at the same time.

I began to go to the Hungarian Reformed church on Sundays where I met a beautiful Hungarian girl named Olivia who'd come to the USA just a few years earlier. Her mother and father had been working in Admiral Horthy's residence in Spain until his death. At that point, they'd made their way to the United States.

I also met a gentleman who was a vice president at General Motors. "Are you interested in going to college?" he asked me.

"Yes," I said. I explained I wanted very much to go to college but didn't see how that would be possible. By that time, I'd only been in the U.S. for a couple of months, and I was just getting my feet under me.

"Can you prove you are a high school graduate?"

"Yes," I said. I had the paperwork to prove I'd finished my studies, even if I'd bailed out on my year of confiscating food and livestock from already-desperate farmers.

As it turned out, the man was a notable alumnus of Wabash College in Crawfordsville, Indiana, and was not only willing, but able, to open the door to my future by arranging a special scholarship for immigrants through General Motors.

The next thing I knew, I was college bound.

"I just met you a few weeks ago and now you will be leaving me already?" Olivia said when she heard the news.

I thought about Elizabeth back in Vienna and felt badly about leaving yet another lovely young lady behind. But, once again, I couldn't pass up such an important opportunity.

WABASH COLLEGE

My English was still rudimentary, so I half assumed I was on my way to college on an Indian reservation as I set out with my alumnus sponsor in a brand new, red 1957 Chevrolet convertible for the 700-mile drive to Crawfordsville, Indiana.

The whole way I thought, *if only my old tribe back in Debrecen could see me now!*

We stopped overnight at the mansion of a rich Hungarian family who had come to the USA just before the First World War. Like me, the father had started out with nothing—no job or money—and had begun to collect junk metal, which he resold to refineries for a meager living until World War II started and the U.S. government needed all the scrap metal they could get their hands on to build tanks, equipment, and ammunition.

Dinner that evening included sterling silver and china with a huge crystal chandelier lighting the room. Then, I was shown to my very own bedroom for the evening. I was exhausted that night, but I couldn't sleep. I spent the evening imagining what I could do and be, and how much money I could make.

If these people could become successful in America, I could too.

The next morning, I enjoyed breakfast with the family, including the couple's two grown sons. They showed me their beautifully landscaped backyard, which was enclosed by an ivy-covered fence. They took me through the back gate where they kept two small airplanes. I simply couldn't believe my eyes. In America, private individuals could not only own airplanes but keep them on their property?

I had witnessed the American Dream in action.

Wabash was a private business college. Since I'd graduated from a bookkeeping technical high school, I felt like I'd be a natural once I bridged the language barrier. Because of the difference between Capitalism and Communism, that couldn't have been further from the truth. In addition, I had a long way to go in terms of communication, seeing as I spoke only a dozen words of English. The whole experience would prove to be wonderful just the same.

I arrived at Wabash in April as their very first foreign student.

Ever.

I was housed in a dormitory for a few weeks. During that time, the fraternities had a contest to see who would "win" me. The next thing I knew, I was Phi Delta Theta and had moved into the fraternity house where I made instant, lifelong friends.

Because the Dean of Foreign Students had only one charge—me—we quickly grew close, and he helped me make a plan to learn English so I could start attending classes by the fall semester.

In addition, he helped me to correspond with the various embassies so I could arrange to get my brother to the United States.

While I had been staying with Tony's family, Istvan had been living at a hotel somewhere in Great Britain while learning to operate machinery for his job as a coal miner. Thankfully, we were able to get him out of there before he ever spent a day working below ground.

Istvan—now Steven—came to Indiana where we had joyful reunion.

Back in Debrecen, he'd been studying to become a cabinet maker, so the dean was able to help him land a job in nearby Indianapolis with a company that made furniture by hand. His sixteen fellow employees were all Europeans!

My parents, to whom I wrote regularly, were overjoyed to learn we were together and thriving. Much of what I said and sent was censored so, at one point, I wrote to the *Voice of America*. When I was still in Hungary, I remembered people living in the West could dedicate a song to certain people and they would say their name as well as the name of who sent the song on the air. My parents later claimed they'd heard their names on the radio, but I was never sure if it was true or simply said to placate me. It didn't matter—as long as we were in communication. It would be years before Steven and I would see them, so I relished sending them everything I could and hearing whatever news from home made it through the unnecessary scrutiny.

Before Steven arrived, the Dean of Foreign Students also took me on field trips. We went to visit the Flying A oil refinery on the outskirts of Indianapolis, the Indianapolis 500 auto race, and other places of note. Of course, the dean had no idea I'd been to Indianapolis with some of the guys from the house— to see risqué shows at the old Vaudeville theater—on more than one weekend!

At the Flying A refinery, we had a guide show us around. When he found out I was Hungarian, he asked me if I'd ever met Mickey Hargitay, Mr. Universe.

"He worked here until he became Mr. Universe. Now he is now in Hollywood."

Hollywood. The word resonated in my head . . .

When I learned there was a student theater organization at Wabash, I made a beeline to their next meeting. In my very broken English, I told them I was very interested in the theater and I'd been an actor since my early teens in Hungary.

The Wabash thespians were getting ready to start rehearsals on a play entitled the *Teahouse of the August Moon.* Because my accent was so thick, I figured I didn't stand a chance of getting on stage, but they welcomed me into their group, and I knew I would learn a lot just by being involved.

When they saw how keen an interest I had, they suggested I take a small part in the play—only four lines. They suggested I could learn my lines phonetically. I happily accepted the offer and was thrilled to begin practicing theater arts in English. At first, I had no idea what I would be saying, but used my Hungarian dictionary to translate the words and learned my lines.

It was a treat to be back on stage.

As a result of my theater experience, I decided to learn fifty English words every day. I figured I'd speak perfectly in weeks.

My efforts lasted two days.

Instead, I began to engage in conversation anywhere I could find it. I had made a lot of friends at the fraternity house, on campus, and everywhere I went. In the beginning, there was a lot of hand gesturing and rudimentary pencil and paper sketches. If I did not know the word or a name for something, I would say, "You know that whatchamacallit?"

I began to (or pretended to) have conversations with all my friends at Phi Delta Theta— even the chef and kitchen helper. I realized they all liked to talk with me, even if it was to laugh at my heavy accent when I answered a question or pretended to understand what they said.

The dean suggested I get the local newspaper, lock myself in a room, and read the articles aloud. It didn't matter whether I understood the words or not.

That turned out to be a very helpful suggestion.

I also took in midwestern American culture with the help of people like Bill, a local boy whose family owned a large farm some distance from campus. He was also a Phi Delta Theta and drove a brand-new Pontiac. He invited me to the farm several times. I understood farms and farming, but I had no idea how large his family farm would be.

I was particularly fascinated by their thirty dairy cows, all of them white with large black or red patches and huge udders. Like my old pal Fancy, these cows were very smart. They put the cows out to pasture for the day. At four in the afternoon, when it was time to come back to the barn, they all followed each other, first into a building where they were washed and dried—much like a car wash only gentler and built just for them. After the shower, they lumbered back to the barn, which was clean like a laboratory, and into their own stalls. Farmworkers put the milking apparatus on their udders and the milking began.

You could actually see the milk flow overhead via clear tubes into the collection area. The cows were not tied into the milking stall, so when the apparatus was taken off, they simply backed out and proceeded to walk into another barn next door, where they spent the night.

Bill also proudly showed me their airplane, a Cessna 172. He explained most larger farms around the state of Indiana had their own airplanes. Some even had the coveted Cessna 310 with two engines. I now understood what I'd seen on my drive to college, but I still couldn't believe an American didn't have to be in the air force to own and fly a plane!

I vowed to get my pilot's license as soon as I had the opportunity.

Wabash was an all-men's college, so finding girls to date was a priority. I was warned the local boys considered us outsiders and dating a local girl often led to big trouble. The remedy was to go to another town to find a date.

"Hey, John (as I was now known), we are going to go to Greencastle to visit Saint Marie's of the Woods school this Sunday." I was asked one day. "Do you want to come?"

"Sure," I said, "but why there?"

"It's a Catholic girl's school and they are having their annual basketball game—the students against the faculty. It's a riot."

"What's so funny about that?"

"The faculty are all nuns, and they play in full uniform, even their headdresses."

"That does sound fun."

"Maybe you'll even meet a nice Catholic girl you can date. The girls there are required to be on campus all week except for on Sundays after noon. If you have a girlfriend there, you have to go early, before noon, to line up with your car to pick them up."

The whole thing sounded crazy, but fun all the same. When we got to the school, I spotted a line of young men outside on the street waiting for their dates. I did, in fact, meet a nice South American girl who was a student there. Her name was Hortenzia, which I found interesting given the fact my father was a horticulturist. He was experimenting with a flower called Hortenzia, which could change color.

My Hortenzia said she felt like she was in a prison at her school.

The relationship was short-lived due to the restrictions we faced to even see each other, but she was beautiful, and I enjoyed her company very much.

I would hear from both Olivia and Elizabeth while I was at Wabash. Olivia came for a visit more than once, and Elizabeth found me and wrote that she wanted to come and live with me in the U.S.

While I had feelings for both young ladies, I wasn't anywhere near ready for that sort of commitment.

I was just discovering how much fun it was to be an American college student.

Freshmen in the fraternity house had it rough at times, especially on their birthdays. To celebrate, they had to go into a cold shower and stay until one of the seniors decided to let them out.

One freshman was a big, well-built guy for his age. When his birthday came around, he went along with the tradition, but only for about half an hour. When he wanted out and was told no, he busted out anyway, got a bucket, and started what turned into a major water fight. In the midst of the pandemonium, someone yelled, "Let's go have a water fight with our neighbors."

Suddenly everyone took their buckets, containers, and water hoses and turned them on the fraternity next door.

A little while later, someone yelled, "Let's go to DePauw!"

DePauw University was the archenemy of Wabash.

Soon, over twenty cars full of Wabash men were headed toward the residence halls and fraternities of our rival school. We knew the territory and picked out the houses with open windows, doors, and garages. We hooked up our hoses to their garden faucets and let them have it.

I was more or less an observer and did not physically participate in the action, except to fill some of the buckets and help with the water hose.

At the sound of police sirens, we all ran to our cars and fled. Our bunch made it, but about half the guys were arrested. The next day, the headline of the Indianapolis newspaper read, "Wabash College Students Arrested at DePauw University."

For the first time, I felt a little like I had when I'd crossed the Hungarian border and escaped into Austria. I certainly wasn't in the same degree of danger, but I definitely didn't want to suffer the consequences of getting caught. I considered myself lucky to have avoided arrest.

Unlike the other students, I had nowhere to go over the summer. To solve the problem, I was offered a job painting the bleachers on the football field. I was also to work on my English so I could start the next year in the fall with the rest of the students.

I got to stay in the Phi Delta Theta house by myself. My diet that summer was all American and consisted of Sugar Puffs cereal, Pepsi Cola, and the occasional hot dog or hamburger. I was determined to save all the money I could, because I wanted to visit New York over the Christmas holiday—I'd been there briefly but wanted to explore the city like a proper American tourist.

When September came, my English was very good, and I was ready to enroll as a regular student with the rest of the 750 students. I could keep up with my classmates; however, it wasn't easy.

The local newspapers wrote about me several times. Because of that, people on campus and in town knew who I was. When I walked down the main street in Crawfordsville, people smiled and said hello. More than once, storekeepers literally pulled me from the sidewalk into their store and gave me a shirt, or a pair of shoes, much like in Vienna. I didn't like it, but I appreciated the help. I wanted to be able to pay for the things I needed. Also, I knew my family back in Hungary didn't have the comfort of a good life, while here people gave me gifts just because they'd heard about me or read about me in the newspaper.

A good friend at Wabash had a Volkswagen Beetle. We drove out to the beautiful countryside around Crawfordsville, and I learned to drive between the corn and the sunflower fields.

He took me to take my driving test and get my driver's license.

What a great feeling that was!

All I needed was a car and I was on my way!

Christmas break came and I had saved up enough money to visit the Big Apple. I really wanted to visit the Statue of Liberty, not as a refugee staring from the deck of a ship, but from the balcony around the torch. Then, I wanted to see Harlem. I knew all about gangsters and the enticing danger from the paperbacks I'd read back in Hungary and needed to experience it myself. I also wanted to a walk on Broadway, which I thought of as the heart of the world.

One of my college buddies took me partway. From there, I bought a bus ticket. He warned me about how expensive the hotels were in New York and advised me to stay at the YMCA on 34th Street. I found the Y easily, and it was affordable—two dollars per night.

The next morning, I went down to the cafeteria for breakfast and had pancakes and tea. As I was eating, I saw a guy two tables away who looked like he could be Hungarian. When I finished my breakfast, I went over to his table and spoke to him in my mother tongue. He replied in German but spoke English as well. It turned out he was also visiting New York for the first time. I told him I really want to go to Harlem to check it out but had heard it was a dangerous place. He said that's where he wanted to go too.

We both assumed we needed to be dressed appropriately, so he said, "Why don't we go find a used clothing store and buy some leather jackets? That will be pretty safe if we get in a fight."

We soon embodied the European ideal of American tough guys and were ready to go! We walked up and down what we thought was the main street in Harlem and passed a bar. The sign up front advertised half a fried chicken, French fries, and a beer for seventy-five cents. Neither of us said anything about it, but when we got hungry, I suggested we check it out. We went inside the dark bar, expecting the worst.

We ordered our food and were served with no incident.

"Let's order another beer and see what happens," I said.

The place was filling up, and most of the patrons were black.

"How are you doin' guys?" the man beside me asked. "Are you in New York for the first time?"

"Here we go," I thought.

As it turned out, the man and his buddies were Merchant Marines who'd just come back from a three-week trip to Europe.

"Where are you from?" he asked.

"Hungary," I said.

"I am from Germany," my friend said.

"We've been there— Bremerhaven," he said.

Everyone in the huge bar turned out to be friendly. The place was a hangout for Merchant Marines who'd come back from sea, and they couldn't have been a nicer bunch. There was absolutely no danger to be found.

I enjoyed every minute that followed on that trip—from walking up and down Broadway to paying an official visit to Lady Liberty.

I was in the heart of the free world

In my second semester, a new Hungarian refugee student, as well as a Greek boy from Athens, were admitted to the school. The Hungarian student's name was Károly, and he turned out to be an excellent artist.

That spring I learned there was an annual alumni get together. On the appointed day, there were, it seemed, hundreds of expensive cars: Cadillacs, Lincolns, and even a Rolls Royce or two parked all over the campus. In other words, a lot of alums had become successful businessmen, and they got together every year to support Wabash College.

Which gave me an idea.

I asked Károly to draw pictures of all the notable old buildings on campus. I figured they would be familiar and nostalgic to these alumni visitors.

Károly did an excellent job of drawing up the individual buildings. With his permission, I took one and went to town to have it copied. It looked as good as the original. I asked him if we could highlight them with watercolor so they looked authentic and told him I planned to sell them to the alums as souvenirs.

"Great idea, but how?" Károly asked.

"I will get their list of names and we'll offer the drawings to them through the mail."

I went to our dean of foreign students. He liked the idea and gave us a list of fifty names. I had Károly make up ten copies of each of the buildings, and then had him enhance them with watercolor.

We did a test mailing and sold a few for a hefty margin, which Károly and I split.

Soon after, we were called into the president's office. He told me there had been complaints and we had to stop our marketing endeavor immediately.

My first try at business in the United States was over.

In retrospect, I should have negotiated by offering to give a percentage of our earnings back to the school or to some college-related charity. I just wasn't sophisticated enough about business to realize that.

Not yet . . .

HEADED WEST

As I got to know my fellow students, I began to realize who these boys were and what prominent families they came from. There were big landowner's sons and the sons of famous lawyers and politicians. They hailed from all different parts of the country, and there were many different characters among them.

One boy invited me to his parents' horse ranch in Kentucky. The whole state was beautiful and green, and the horses were magnificent. I was invited to dinner with the family. One of the main courses looked to me like fried chicken but was somehow tastier. After dinner, my friend lit up a cigar with his father who asked, "Did you like the main course?"

"Yes, of course. It was delicious."

"Did you know what it was?"

"Yes, fried chicken," I said.

"Bullfrog," he said.

I was lucky I didn't throw up right there, but I did like hanging out with them. My friend was cool with his cigars and the wad of money he always had with him. Besides being in his third year at Wabash, he was a gambler. In his free time, he went to Chicago and gambled at the horse track.

One day, he asked me if I wanted to go with him.

"I appreciate that, but I don't have extra money to lose."

"I'll give you two dollars, and I'll show you what horse to bet on. You'll win, you'll see."

We went and I won four dollars.

My friend said he was going into a special club for higher-stakes betting. While he was gone, greed got the better of me and I put all four dollars on a horse. I won again and had eight dollars to my name.

"Heck," I thought. "This is easy."

That was until I gambled again and lost it all.

Andy came from a family of doctors and professionals. He was a third-year student and came from Amish Country. One spring break, he took me to his family summer house by Diamond Lake. We had a great time frolicking in the crystal-clear water which had a perfectly round island in the middle with a large house on it.

"How do the residents get on and off the island?" I asked.

"They have a butler who takes them back and forth from their private dock not far from here."

I was enchanted and amazed at how people lived in my new country.

I met a second-year student named Jack in one of my classes and we became good friends. His grandfather was the former governor of Indiana, but he was from California.

"I just love it back home," he said.

"What city are you from?" I asked.

"Los Angeles," he said.

"That's where Hollywood is, right?"

"Yes," said Jack. "I'm organizing a trip back there this summer. We have room in the car for one more person. Why don't you come?"

"Where will I stay?" I asked.

"I'll tell my parents you're a friend from school and we'll figure something out for you."

"Do they still have a lot of gold mines there?" I asked.

"Probably some," he said with a laugh. "But it is a very different world now. We'll travel on Route 66. You'll love it. It's like a living museum. The new highways General Eisenhower is having built are up to six lanes. They may be good for the economy, but Route 66 is the way to go if you want to see the real America."

I didn't want to be a burden, but Jack assured me it would be no problem.

Real America was everything and nothing like I expected.

To me, Texas represented individualism and conjured up my romantic notions of cowboys and Indians. The men who made Texas famous were the pioneers and carpetbaggers who settled there. They built vast ranches and made Texas the biggest state in the United States of America.

When we got there, it was very hot, almost unbearably so. We drove through town after typical town, many with old gas stations that still sold gas from the Model-T days. These old stations had one pump where you syphoned up the gas by moving an arm back and forth into a glass cylinder. When you had enough gas, you opened a spigot on the side of the pump and the gas disappeared into your tank from the cylinder.

Another little town had a public swimming pool, and the whole town seemed to be there trying to cool off.

"Full house," the cashier said when we tried to go in.

Hot and annoyed, we drove around to the back, changed into swim trunks, and climbed the wire fence one at a time, all for the chance to dip into lukewarm water warmed by the sun and hundreds of people.

It was less than refreshing.

We were driving through yet another small town when we spotted cowboys coming out of a storefront.

"It's a bar," someone said.

"I want to go inside and see," I said.

We all went in, and I found myself in a place right out of the movies complete with sawdust, spittoons, and a bar with no seats. There was even a brass footrail so you could lean in and order a drink. The bartender was in full cowboy garb and had a real six shooter hanging at his side. So did the rest of the cowboys, all with sunburned, rugged faces and cowboy boots with spurs. It was just like I'd imagined from my black-market western paperbacks.

"My God," I thought. "I am in the real Texas!"

The only thing missing were the Native Americans I so longed to meet.

We drove by several major road-building crews constructing the Eisenhower highways. My buddies took all the construction—including the elaborate machines the road crews used—for granted. I was the only excited one in the bunch. I simply couldn't understand how they could doze off with giant machines spitting out concrete and creating infrastructure I couldn't even have imagined back in Hungary.

As I gazed out at endless desert as far as the eye could see, I found it hard to believe we were nearly in California

"Look ahead," I said. "There is a roadblock."

"It's the California border checkpoint."

"I thought California was part of the United States," I said.

"Yes," Jack said, "but you'll learn California is different from the rest of the country. If we have fruit in the car, they will take it away and throw it in the trash can."

"You mean they confiscate it? Really? I thought this was a free country and they didn't take away anything that's private."

"A lot of fruit and vegetables are grown in California, and they don't want you to bring in harmful insects or anything that would be detrimental to the agriculture."

I had no fruit on me, but I was still nervous. There were several uniformed men at the checkpoint, and I was all too familiar with what could happen.

One officer came to the car and looked in.

"Where are you gentlemen coming from?" he asked.

Before anyone in the car could answer, I said from the back seat, "We came from Indiana on Route 66."

The man smiled at my accent and asked. "Are you gentleman carrying any fruit in the car?"

Some of the guys had bananas and grapes, so we placed all the fruit we had into a wastebasket.

"Thank you," he said. "Welcome to California from Indiana."

He saluted and allowed us to pass through.

I couldn't believe that was all there was to it.

"Where is all this agriculture they are protecting?" I asked as we pressed on.

"Further north."

"Where they mine all the gold?"

"There is not much of that being done, nowadays."

Clearly, I had a lot to learn.

Soon, a big dry lake appeared on the horizon. We stopped to rest, get gas, and check the oil. While we were there, we enjoyed the shade under a canopy at what I learned was the great salt lake of Southern California.

"Palm Springs is coming up shortly," Jack said.

"What is there in Palm Springs?" I asked.

"Big houses, lots of rich people, and movie stars like Frank Sinatra."

"The singer!" I said.

"Alright! You are becoming an American."

"Can we stop for a look around?" I asked, spotting palm trees and beyond eager to get my first glimpse of the celebrity lifestyle.

"We'll come back, and I'll show you the town at some point this summer," Jack said. "My parents are expecting us in Los Angeles before dark and we're not too far away. We just have to go through that canyon between those mountains ahead. When we come out on the other end, we'll be close to Whittier, the suburb where I'm from."

My first thought about Los Angeles was that it was even smoggier than I'd imagined.

Jack's parents met us, and we transferred from our buddies' car into their Cadillac.

They had arranged for me to stay with some family friends and drove me over to where I would be living. We entered a driveway that led up the side of a hill. At the end of the driveway were two houses, one very large and the other quite a bit smaller. The owner, his wife, and their two daughters came out to greet us.

"Welcome," they said and pointed to the smaller house. "Make yourself comfortable in our guest house."

Jack and his family left, and my generous summer sponsors led me into a lovely little house that truly had every comfort I could imagine.

"Rest up, take a shower, and come on up to the house for dinner at seven."

After a nice dinner followed by a good night's sleep, Jack reappeared the next morning. He was giddy like he'd fallen in love with the most beautiful girl in the world. Except it wasn't a girl that had caught his eye, but the brand new MGB sports car his parents had bought for him as a homecoming gift.

A gift just for coming home? I was still thinking like a kid who'd escaped from behind the Iron Curtain, but I really couldn't believe it. I was happy for him though, because I knew he and I would be driving all over town with the top down.

By 3:00 p.m., we were completely sunburned from a day filled with freeways and sunshine.

"Hey Jack, I need a car too," I said as he dropped me off. "But it has to be cheap. I only have sixty dollars."

"I'll see what I can do," he said.

When I went into my place, my skin was on fire, but there was a note from my sponsor inviting me up to the main house for dinner again.

"So, what is your plan here in California?" he asked as we ate.

"I was thinking I'd get a summer job to make some money to pay for a car and rent a short-term place to stay."

The father was impressed by my ambition, so he called a friend who owned a tortilla factory and willing to hire me.

"What is a tortilla factory?" I asked.

"It's like bread for the Mexican people," he said with a smile. "Tortillas are very popular in California."

"Thank you for helping me find this job," I said.

Then, the phone rang.

"I think we found you a car," said Jack.

"Really? Already?"

"It's a black, four-door, 1940 Oldsmobile with a flathead six-cylinder engine. It's got running boards on both sides. Apparently, it looks like a gangster car from the movies. It belonged to someone who was in the war and never returned. It's been parked in my friend Dale's garage for a while. Dad and I are going to see it this afternoon and I'll let you know about it later."

"Great," I said. "Thanks for finding it."

"I'll introduce you to the owner of the tortilla factory in the morning," my sponsor said after I'd hung up.

In one day, I had both a job and car on the horizon.

The car definitely turned out to be something out of a Hollywood gangster film—all black with a long hood. It was nice, clean, and mechanically sound. On top of that, Jack's longtime friend Dale told me I could have it for $40. We became friends, and I became the proud owner of a 1940 Oldsmobile. I registered it in my name at the California DMV.

The Tortilla Factory was a small outfit with twelve employees, most of whom were Mexican ladies who didn't speak English. They manufactured tortillas, put them in bags, labeled them, and boxed them up for delivery. A small truck delivered the tortillas to retail outfits all over the city. Because the tortillas were made of corn and they fermented the corn for days, the place had an awful smell. I knew the job wasn't for me right from the start, but I needed the money for my car and a place to live, so I got right down to work.

When I wasn't working, I was out exploring in my new car. Whittier was a nice city, but it was a bedroom community. People commuted to Los Angeles and lived in Whittier. In other words, it was way too far away from the action.

I made my way into Hollywood to have a look at the studios: Warner Brothers, Columbia, Universal, Twentieth Century Fox, and Paramount. I drove into Beverly Hills. At the city limit, on the Sunset Boulevard side, there was a sign on the grass between the curb and the sidewalk advertising maps and tours to the movie stars' homes.

I saw tourists pulling over to buy a map or inquire as to when the next tour would start. I had a feeling that the person selling maps and tours had a lot of information I wanted, so I turned around and parked. It took me a few minutes, but I finally got up the courage to get out of my car and ask him some questions.

"Do you actually go into the actor's houses or just drive by and tell the people who lives there and some of their history?"

"Why? Do you want to go on one of my tours?" he asked.

"I don't have the money for that. I'm just very curious about actors and Hollywood in general."

In between my rapid-fire questions he would yell, "Movie stars' home tour starts here!" or, "Buy a map to the movie stars' homes!"

"How did these stars start their careers?" I asked.

"They had natural talent, or they perfected their skills at drama school. From there, they got an agent. The lucky ones got work or a contract with a studio. That's how they become rich and famous."

I nodded along.

"Why are you asking me all these questions? Do you want to be an actor?"

"I am just curious about the film industry," I said, too embarrassed to admit I did. "By the way are you looking for someone to work for you in your business?"

"Not today, kid," he said. "But stop by and ask me again some time."

HOORAY FOR HOLLYWOOD
1962

My career packaging tortillas lasted for one week. Not only did the place smell horrible, but I was the only gringo. My co-workers were friendly, but I could not learn or develop my English amongst people who didn't speak the language either. Besides, I wanted to be closer to the action. I collected my week's pay and used it to pay my way on an excursion Dale organized down to Mexico.

There were four of us traveling in a 1953 Pontiac, and it was a truly international coalition. Dale was the American, Ricardo was from Barcelona, Franz was from Vienna, and I was from Hungary. All of us were university students in the USA, but Ricardo and Franz were headed back to their respective countries after the trip.

Every time we stopped in a Mexican village bar for a little refreshment, we would have a near battle between Ricardo and the Mexicans. Whenever anyone asked us where we were from, I would say Budapest, Franz would say Vienna, Dale would say Los Angeles, and Ricardo would say Barcelona. When Ricardo would say Barcelona, it was with his tongue halfway hanging out of his mouth. One would always have to be ready with a napkin or handkerchief.

The Mexicans would smile and repeat the word Barcelona the way they pronounced it in Mexican Spanish with an "s" sound.

Ricardo would repeat the name of his city the Spanish way.

The Mexican would say it his or her way, and Ricardo, a proud Spaniard, could not accept what he considered to be improper Spanish from someone in the colonies.

Sometimes it would go on until one of us would step in.

We went all the way to Mexico City where Ricardo's uncle owned three hotels. We were his guests for a few days. When we were watching television in the lobby of the hotel, I was very surprised to see my favorite American TV programs in Spanish—incorrect Spanish according to Ricardo.

Upon my return, it was time to get another job.

I planned to head directly to Hollywood but took a slight detour into Beverly Hills and landed a gig as a bellhop at the Beverly Hills Hotel. I was to be paid a small salary and what promised to be big tips. The hotel was a haven for the wealthy and powerful and had a number of bungalows in the back where famous people lived for extended periods of time, including Elizabeth Taylor and Howard Hughes. Since I'd be working with rich people figured I'd make a fortune in a couple of months.

I figured wrong.

When a car or taxi pulled up to the hotel, I was instructed not to touch the luggage until the bell captain told me where to take it. The bell captain had it all worked out so he could take the luggage out of the vehicle and get the tip for his service while I dragged the suitcases to the rooms.

As a result, I never got a dime in tips.

I worked for two weeks and quit.

I still needed to be employed, even for a short time, so I applied for a job at the Standard Oil Company gas station on the corner of Little Santa Monica Boulevard and Canon Drive. I was hired, trained, and given a uniform which included a white shirt, pants, and hat.

I clocked in starting the following Monday, so with a few days off, I went apartment hunting. I found a furnished one bedroom on 141 South Elm Drive in Beverly Hills for $105 per month. Seeing as my salary was to be $425, I was well within my budget.

I went back to my guest cottage, packed my bag, and thanked my sponsors for allowing me to stay with them. I promised I'd come back to say goodbye before I went back to Indiana at the end of summer.

Next, I opened the telephone book in search of an agent. I found an agency located nearby, went in, and told the receptionist I was new in town and would like to speak with an agent.

She smiled and picked up the phone. A few minutes later she said, "Second door on the right."

I walked right in, introduced myself, and sat down.

"Do you have headshots?" the agent asked.

"No," I replied.

"You have an accent. Where are you from?"

"I am Hungarian," I told him. "I came to this country in 1957 and am in college in Indiana.

"So, you want to be an actor for three months and then go back to school?"

I nodded.

"That's going to be a bit difficult," he said with a smile. "How much acting experience do you have?"

"I did some things in Hungary, and I was in *The Tea House in the August Moon* at college," I said proudly.

"What you should do is find out if you can transfer your credits from your college in Indiana to UCLA and see if UCLA would accept you into their film school. That is, if you really want to be an actor. Also, there are a lot of small theaters around where you can do plays to gain experience. If you do, you are much more likely to find an agent who will sign you up and represent you at the studios."

I appreciated that he took the time to explain the system to me. On his advice, I went over to UCLA. They gave me instructions about how to have my paperwork and credentials sent and indicated they would decide from there.

Excited, I called the Dean of Foreign Students at Wabash and asked him about the possibility of transferring my credentials to UCLA. Seeing as it was summer, he said it would take a few days but to call him back.

Four days went by quickly. I called him back expecting good news.

"John," he said. "As it turns out, you have a special scholarship from General Motors. They expect you to go to work for them when you graduate from Wabash, so a transfer is not possible."

I'd honestly had no idea how my college was being paid for and what stipulations were attached. "Thank you for that information. I guess I'll be heading back to Crawfordsville in the fall."

I was both appreciative and incredibly disappointed.

Working at Standard Oil in Beverly Hills turned out to be a joyful experience. When a car pulled in for gas, four of us jumped on it. The first guy put in the fuel—regular or super, per the customer's request. The next attendant checked the air pressure, the third guy cleaned the windows, and the fourth opened the hood to check the water in the radiator and the battery.

Across the street, on lower Santa Monica Blvd, was a stock exchange. A lot of the people who worked there got their cars serviced by us. In addition, almost every day, at least one recognizable film star pulled in for gas. Doris Day's son and his friends came to the station a lot. He asked a lot of questions about my 1940 Oldsmobile, which caused a stir everywhere I went. In fact, I felt like something of a celebrity when I drove around in it.

One afternoon, a Lincoln convertible stalled halfway into the driveway of the station. The driver was trying to restart the car but to no avail. I walked over to see if I could help.

"The damn thing ran out of gas!" the driver said in a Hungarian accent.

The driver was none other than Mickey Hargitay, Mr. Universe! The very same man the tour guide mentioned when the dean and I visited in Indianapolis.

"Let's push it to the pump together," he said.

Mickey Hargitay was so muscular he could have picked up the whole car and carried it to the pumps all by himself, but I said, "Okay!"

I looked back and saw Ray the assistant manager looking at us. Ray was from Kentucky and spoke with a funny accent. He had a very thin body—no muscles at all with stick-thin arms you could see because his shirt sleeves were always turned up above his elbows.

"Hey, Ray," I yelled. "Come help us push this car to the pumps."

Ray was about one-third Mickey Hargitay's size, but he came over. We both thought Mickey would help us. Instead, the man just stood there while the two of us tried but couldn't get the car to budge.

"We need more help," Mickey said.

Two other attendants came over and we managed to push the car to the pumps.

As it turned out Mr. Universe was something of a weakling. He was a nice guy though, and as I handled the pump and started to fill it up, we had a nice conversation in Hungarian. He seemed happy to be able to speak his native language. I definitely was. Of all people, I couldn't believe I'd met him.

About two hours later, I saw his car again, top down, with a blond lady in the passenger seat. He pulled back into the station. The lady was his wife, Jayne Mansfield.

I'll never forget what she was wearing, not that there was much to it—a tight, low cut pink angora sweater that did little to contain her ample cleavage. Surprisingly, she had no makeup on, so I saw all her freckles. She was absolutely beautiful.

"I told her about you, and she made me drive down here to meet you," Mickey said.

Jayne Mansfield was ecstatic to meet another Hungarian and promptly started trying out her Hungarian on me. A lot of the words she'd learned were expletives!

They stayed for a good ten minutes.

As they left, she waved goodbye.

Needless to say, I was the station hero from that day on.

Fall was coming fast, and I didn't want to leave California. If I went back to Wabash and finished school, I'd have a great job. Maybe I'd rise in the automobile industry and become a vice president. It sounded great. Not at all adventurous, but certainly safe. If I stayed in California, I would be entirely on my own, but I would learn more about how the film and television business worked.

I'd read that when oil was discovered in the U.S., very few people saw the possibilities because there were no cars yet. John D. Rockefeller, however, found a use for it. At that time, they had wax to make candles but were still burning whale oil for light. Rockefeller went and gave away lanterns for free to people if they used his oil from the ground to create light.

Entrepreneurship—I liked that word.

To me, it meant that if I invented something or created something, took a little risk, and worked like hell, the glory could be mine. I had a sense of freedom like I'd never experienced to make whatever choice I wanted to. I did not have to be in the Communist party to become an actor or anything else. I didn't have to worry about the government or political parties. In America, I had independence and freedom to be an entrepreneur.

Because my immediate ambition was the film industry, specifically, the acting world, I called the Dean of Foreign Students once more to persuade him to make it a reality for me to go to UCLA film school.

"I tried, John," he said. "The scholarship won't allow it."

I thought about it for a few more days and decided to stay in California anyway.

I wrote a nice letter to the school, called my friend Jack to let him know I wouldn't be driving back with him, and explained my decision to my fraternity house buddies too.

Then I called my brother Istvan, now Steven, back in Indiana. It was my mother's wish that we be together, so I invited him to come and live with me in Beverly Hills.

He agreed to come.

My brother and I set up camp together at 141 Elm Drive. We got him a good job in a small cabinet shop where he made filigrees out of wood. My 1940 Oldsmobile was working great, even if I was afraid to take it on long trips. In town, it got lots of attention. Still, I wanted a more modern car—a convertible so I could enjoy the California sun.

My wish came true one morning when I started up my Oldsmobile and put it in reverse. It didn't move. The reverse gear had gone out. I talked with a few mechanics, but no one would work on it because they couldn't get the parts for it anymore. I called the closest junkyard and told them I had a 1940 Oldsmobile. They said they would pay $10 dollars for it and haul it away.

In its place, I bought a used Ford Fairlane convertible.

When I went to work at the gas station a few days later, Doris Day's son and his buddies showed up.

"Where is your car?" they asked.

I pointed to my lovely Ford Fairlane convertible.

"No, the other one."

"I sold it."

"What?" the three of them shouted in unison.

"How much did you get for it?"

"Ten bucks," I said happily.

"Are you kidding? We were going to offer you $750 for it."

"Are you guys kidding?"

"You don't know what you had there. We'd have gone up to $1000."

"I had a car with no reverse gear that couldn't be fixed," I said.

"What you had was a collector's item."

"Who would collect an old car like that?" I asked.

"We researched your car. It was built in 1940 and they only built 600 of them because all the car factories turned to make tanks, air-planes, and equipment for the war. If we rebuilt and repainted it, that car would be worth $25,000."

All I could say was, "Really?"

The boys left disappointed. I heard one say to the other, "I told you guys we should have bought that car. Now we missed a good opportunity. That guy didn't even understand how valuable it was."

"Oh well," I said. "I guess my grandpa was right. One always learns, and yet they die not knowing."

SUNSET BOULEVARD

I worked at the gas station for about a year. During that time, I tried to pick up everything I could about becoming a successful American businessman including catchphrases like *buy low/sell high*. My dream was still to be a successful actor.

Not long after, I went into a liquor store on Sunset Boulevard and saw three actors I recognized. My father once said, "People will judge you by who your friends are." If I really wanted to be an actor, I needed to make friends with other actors. I needed to move among them to learn all they knew. That section of Sunset was part of the famous Sunset Strip, in other words, just where I wanted to be.

I asked for a job and was hired to be a delivery man.

My job was to deliver liquor orders in the store van for King's Cellar. They also had another store on Sunset and Clark called Angel's Corner. Some orders consisted of a few bottles, and sometimes I delivered several cases of various alcohol items to homes in a delivery area that encompassed Hollywood, the Hollywood Hills, Beverly Hills, and Bel Air.

Every day at about 11:00 a.m., a Harley Davidson pulled up in front of the store and parked in the red zone. The driver, a well-known California Highway Patrol officer, would come in and help himself to a pack of cigarettes, a chocolate bar, or a soft drink. He

217

would stay for ten or fifteen minutes and shoot the breeze with the owners. He was a big, rugged, sunburned guy with a gun hanging on his side. Unlike most highway patrol officers who rode in pairs, he rode alone. Since he patrolled the area, and we were friendly to him, he never ticketed other King's Cellar customers who parked in the red zone. As a result of the accessible parking, not to mention the location, King's Cellar was the liquor store to stop in for the entertainment industry. Movie stars, television actors, directors, producers—they all seemed to know the owner, Harry. They would place their orders, and I was to deliver them to their homes.

Unlike a star homes tour, I was not only getting paid to meet celebrities in the store, but I got to drive behind the gates of all their magnificent abodes and, often, go inside to deliver the boxes!

Needless to say, I liked my job.

The store had an order for a case of liquor and chocolates ready to be delivered in Beverly Hills. The manager gave me the invoice with the address. The customer's name was Arlene Dahl.

I just stared at her name. I was going to the home of one of the most beautiful women in the world. Really?

"Don't forget to come back, John," the manager said and smiled. "We are busy today."

I arrived at the address, got her order out of the van, walked up her manicured front lawn and rang the doorbell.

There was no answer.

I rang again.

A minute later, the door opened and there was Arlene in a sexy nightgown made of white fur and lace.

I almost dropped the box.

"Bring it upstairs, please," she said.

My legs trembled as I followed her into a gigantic bedroom.

"Put it there and I'll get a check for you," she said.

As she went to a writing table, I stood there nearly paralyzed. I had to be imagining what was happening. Could I really be standing in the bedroom with a lingerie-clad female who was one of the most gorgeous women in the world?

"Thank you," she said, handing me payment for the delivery.

"No, thank you," I said.

As I walked down the stairs and out to my van, I was half in love and twice as determined to make my dream of becoming an actor into reality.

I was sure I was dreaming when the truest of all Americans, at least in my eyes, stopped by the store. I'd only ever seen him on the big screen doling out double-barreled truth and justice.

In other words, John Wayne himself strolled in!

I didn't get to speak to him, but it was a moment I'd never forget.

A gentleman came into the store wanting a bottle of gin. As he paid for it and turned to leave, Harold, my manager came out from the back.

"Do you know who that was?" he asked.

"No," I said.

"That's Stewart Stern, the guy who wrote *Rebel Without a Cause*. You know, with James Dean?"

Exactly the sort of person I had taken this job to meet.

A few weeks later, Stewart Stern put in an order and wanted it delivered to his house in the Hollywood Hills.

As I placed the large delivery box in his kitchen and was waiting for the check, I said, "Somebody told me you wrote the screenplay for *Rebel Without a Cause*."

"Tell Harold pretty soon I'll have to pay him for being my publicity agent."

"I'll do that," I said with a smile.

Stewart Stern was a prolific screenwriter who not only wrote *Rebel Without a Cause*, but *Rachel-Rachel, The Ugly American, The Outsider,* and *No Tricks in My Pocket*.

"You have an accent. It sounds Hungarian," he said. "My ancestors are Hungarian."

As it turned out, Stewart Stern was also related to the Lowe's Movie Theatre chain founder and Adolf Zukor, who founded Paramount Studios. "I have a few friends coming up for dinner soon, but the next time you come up let's chat a little bit about that."

Bingo! I thought.

The next time I delivered liquor to his house, Stewart asked me a lot of questions about the Hungarian Revolution of 1956. I was happy to engage in conversation with him. Stewart asked me if I would come to dinner at his house the next night. His friends Joanne Woodward and Paul Newman would be there too!

Not only did I accept an invitation for which I had just delivered the liquor order, but I had a wonderful evening. Joanne Woodward was lovely, and Paul Newman was very friendly, although his eyes were watery and an unnerving shade of very light blue. The conversation was lively and centered on the 1956 Hungarian Revolution and my experiences during that time.

About two weeks later, I got a call from Stewart. Paul Newman and Marlon Brando had asked him to write a segment about the Revolution for a two-hour television special that centered around the Atomic Bomb. The two men planned to go around the world interviewing politicians as well as everyday people on the street as a demonstration against nuclear warfare. This would be a highly political project stemming from ordinary people worldwide but would require U.S. State Department cooperation.

"Will they allow such a project?" I asked.

"I don't know," said Stewart. "You know the Cold War is not really a cold war, and the world is very dangerous. We don't know how the State Department will react. I will write a presentation for Marlon and Paul, and they will present it and discuss it with the proper people in Washington D.C."

He asked me to write down what I'd been through in Hungary during the Revolution so he could use it in his script. I agreed and recounted my experiences in a piece called "Darkness in Debrecen," which I gave to Stewart Stern. The project never got off the ground, but I was proud to have been asked to contribute.

The Angel's Corner store was short a deliveryman, so the owners asked me to work there for a few days. Angel's Corner was a much smaller store, a lot less busy, and had more walk-in customers than King's Cellar.

I was arranging some bottles and overheard one of the regulars chatting with the salesperson.

"I won't be in for a while because I'm going to Spain. We are making several pictures there, and I don't know what to do with my place. I need to find some decent people to rent it while I'm gone."

"Where do you live?" I asked from an aisle over.

"She lives up the hill on Clark," the salesman told me.

"Can I come up there later and take a look?" I asked.

After she left, my co-worker gave me the address and explained how to get up there. "The street is pretty steep, but there's an incredible view of Los Angeles, especially at night."

The woman's home turned out to be beautiful and interesting. There was a little pond with water lilies and goldfish and a curved bridge that led to a Japanese-style house. The home itself was small, but more than adequate for me and my brother.

She offered us a very good monthly rent and had her attorney write up a contract. Our new landlady trusted us because, as she put it, "You are not Hollywood types. God bless them, they come here from all over the world, especially all parts of the United States to become stars. A lot of them just ruin their lives hoping."

I didn't tell her I had the same ambition and moved up there as soon as I could. Steven moved in after our lease ran out on the Elm apartment.

The place was sheer heaven. As it turned out, we were in the middle of an artist's colony and everyone on the block did something for the studios. There was even an acting coach down the street. I could walk down to the famous Whiskey A Go Go on the Sunset Strip where, once, after waiting in line for an hour, I watched Steve McQueen and his entourage walk past a line of almost fifty people and enter.

Well, I thought. If you're a star, you're the star!

BREAK A LEG

The whole time I worked on Sunset, I kept thinking about the agent's advice to get headshots, go to UCLA Film School, and develop my talent. As it turned out, I couldn't afford the tuition, but what I could do was to find those little theaters he'd talked about and try to get parts in productions. If I did well, maybe a film producer would see and hire me.

I found a little place on Melrose called the Horseshoe Theater, which was designed for actors to hone their skills. I went in to see a play there and knew it was a place agents, directors, and producers frequented to find talent for their projects.

While I was there, I was cast as the lead in *The Immoralist* by André Gide, a role James Dean had played on Broadway. I liked deep drama and I loved being in this play. It was always fascinating for me that I could, with the right words, cause total silence in the audience. Sometimes, after a good monologue, I held onto the quiet a little longer than necessary, just to see and or hear the impact the monologue or scene made.

Thinking my European accent might help me to get the part, a friend told me he'd heard they were casting for a play called *Lady of the Camellias*, a French story. I got the part of Gaston, which was a good role. The lead was Max Baer Junior, the son of the famous boxer. This was a well-financed production, but none of the actors were paid. Still, everyone performed like they were making a million dollars.

Max Baer had some actor friends who'd come back from Italy where they worked a lot in the Westerns being made there. One of the actors' names was John Philip Law. He actually made his career in Italy. John was friends with a British actress who very much reminded me of Jayne Mansfield but was even more busty. John and his friend, both American actors, had come back from Italy to look at a script they were being considered for. The British actress came just to scope out possibilities in Hollywood.

Max Baer invited all of us to dinner at the famous Scandia restaurant on the Sunset Strip, a place to see and be seen.

When our car pulled up under the restaurant canopy, we piled out, and the attendant took the car. The whole idea of valet parking gave me an idea I would soon put to good use, but that night was all about show business.

Inside the restaurant, everyone looked up when we walked in, likely because they recognized John Philip Law. We all stepped aside and let the lady slide into the middle of our booth first. She scooted in bosom first and managed to knock the table settings onto the floor with her cleavage. We were the center of attention as the waiter rushed over to rearrange everything.

It was a perfect, if inadvertent, publicity stunt!

Not only was the Scandia restaurant the place to see and be seen, but it was also the spot where the Screen Actors Guild held their annual blood drive. As a member from 1962 to 1985, I went there to donate. After giving blood, the donors went to another room at Scandia and were treated to beverages and a light lunch.

While there, I was introduced to the actress who'd played the female lead in *Sayonara* opposite Marlon Brando. Her name was Miko Taka, and she was an Japanese-American actress from Seattle. After some conversation, she said she was going to be a judge in a beauty contest in Long Beach. They needed two more judges and she invited me to take part in the event with her.

I said yes.

"I'll give you a call when the time comes," she said.

On the day of the event, she came up to my Japanese style house, which she loved, and we went down to Long Beach together to the beauty pageant. I was proud of my association with Miko Taka and when people thought we were an item, I, of course, never argued with them.

I was also honored to be asked to entertain at the Motion Picture Country Home for retired actors with Cesar Romero and others.

I hired and fired several Hollywood agents because I could not find one who believed in me enough to not just represent me but educate me about the business of acting.

Thankfully, Warner Brothers had an opportunity where actors could sign up to do a three-to-five-minute scene along with a partner for the studio's talent directors. They held these tryouts every three weeks at a small stage with about twenty seats.

All the directors and producers knew about these presentations. When they were looking for some particular type of talent, they would come into the Warner Brothers Mini Theater. These tryouts often resulted in parts on TV shows, so I used the opportunity every time I had the chance.

One time, I was in the office of Saly Banayo, the Warner Brother's talent director, auditioning with an actress.

He said, "Okay, start!"

As we did, he took out an electric shaver and began to shave his face. We did our entire three-minute scene over the electric buzz, and then waited for him to respond.

He finally said, "Okay, you guys can come to the Warner Brothers mini theater and try again for the right audience."

It was an annoying situation, but I landed a job working with Peter Falk as a result. At that time, Peter was a New York actor who'd decided to try his luck in Hollywood. We both got parts on an episode of *Alfred Hitchcock Presents*. In fact, we were put in the same dressing room. This was long before he got *Columbo* and he must have needed money because as we were both changing out of our own clothes into our characters' wardrobes, Peter's shirt was slit in back from the neck almost to his waist.

I never said a word about it and neither did he.

We became fast friends.

According to my relatives back in Hungary, Peter Falk was of Hungarian descent. In 1848, after losing the war against the Hapsburgs, Hungary wanted to break away from the Austrian-Hungarian Empire. Hungary had lost against the Austrians after the Austrians made a deal with the Russians to send 200,000 soldiers from the east. Kossuth Lajos, the President of Hungary, came to the United States to ask for help to win the war. He spoke to the Senate and Congress. The Hungarian reporter who accompanied Kossuth Lajos to the U.S. to document the event was actually Peter Falk's relative.

The irony was not lost on me about participating in a scene with a fellow Hungarian actor in a scene not unlike the time I pretended to be covered in blood to scare my sister. This time however, I got whacked on the head with a papier-maché fire log and the blood was made of chocolate syrup.

In the mid-sixties, the Hungarian government finally gave my parents permission to visit—one at a time, to ensure they wouldn't defect.

My mother came first.

Both Steven and I were overcome with tears when she stepped off the plane at LAX. It had been over ten years. We hugged for the first time in what felt like forever. SO much had changed for us, and the first thing we noticed was how different she—a Hungarian lady from behind the Iron Curtain—was dressed. The next day, we took her shopping for a brand new wardrobe.

She was thrilled, and so were we to be able to do that for her after she'd done so much for us.

At that time, I was working on an episode of *The Gomer Pyle Show*. All the cast members wanted to meet and speak with her, so I took her with me to the studio every day.

My name was printed on a director's chair where I sat until I had to go in front of the camera. She looked at my name many times and was as proud as she could possibly be.

"Nice people, huh?" I said after a few days on the set.

"Yes," she said. "Very nice."

Jim Nabors, the star of the show, had a beautiful operatic singing voice. Whenever he had time off from the show he performed in Las Vegas.

"I'll be at the Riviera doing a show in a couple of weeks," he said. "Why don't you bring your mom there to see it? I'll have a couple of tickets for you, of course."

Excited for the opportunity, Mother and I went to Las Vegas, picked up our tickets at will call, and went into the theater. We gave the tickets to the usher, and she led us all the way down to the middle of the front row—the best seats in the house.

The show started, Jim Nabors came out with a big orchestra, and he began to sing. After a few numbers, he came down to stage center, sat down at the edge, and sang an entire song directly to my mother. There were a thousand people in the audience, and the star of the show was gazing right at my mother.

At the end, I asked her, "Do you still think actors are immoral?"

"No," she said. "Go ahead and be an actor."

She talked about her moment with Jim Nabors for the rest of her life.

When it was time for her to return to Hungary, Mother did so without issue. As a result, the government allowed her to come out again, a year later. Because my mother came out twice and went back to Hungary on time, they eventually allowed my father to visit as well.

Finally, they allowed our parents to come together and stay with us for nearly a year. My mother returned a little earlier than my father because she missed my two sisters, Irén and Zita, and her grandchildren in Hungary.

Hungary was home for them.

During one of their visits, I was also able to take my father to watch me tape a show. This time, we were on location for *Here Come the Brides*, the story of three brothers living on a ranch out on the prairie. Robert Brown played the oldest brother, David Soul the middle brother, and Bobby Sherman played the youngest. Joan Blondel also starred.

My father was with me all day and was very interested in how these television shows come to be. He was very proud of how I'd come to America, learned the language, and made my way into television in just a few years.

"This is definitely the land of opportunity and the land of the free," he said. "But do these actors have real jobs, too?"

I appeared in one film, *The Franc Liszt Story*, at Columbia and starring Dirk Bogart. Capuchine, a French model, played his wife. The film was directed by George Cukor, a famous director, of Hungarian descent. I continued to get parts in television series episodes like *Jack Webb's True*, and many others. In my mind, progress was slow. I was not able to get a recurring or starring role. Everyone told me I had to pay my dues to get on a TV series as a regular. That I needed to be patient . . .

I was losing patience.

LIFE IN THE FAST LANE

Not one acting professional ever complained about my work on stage or in the studio. Other actors would say, "You're working so much, your time will come." They also suggested when I wasn't working I should collect unemployment to keep me going.

I went and signed up at the Hollywood unemployment office. Hundreds of recognizable actors were in line, all of whom routinely collected these checks between jobs. For me, once was enough and I never went back.

The film industry was changing. Very few actors were under contract at the studios any longer. That system was coming to an end and independent productions were in vogue. The studios would rent the production companies whatever they needed, and the products would be released under the studio name.

I could have continued to make a meager living like thousands of actors, but I couldn't do it by living on unemployment between gigs. It just didn't feel right to me. I needed to find an agent who would take my representation seriously, or I needed to figure out a way to make enough money to make my own films in which I could star.

In the meantime, I had my eye on the various valet parking operations around Hollywood and Beverly Hills. People drove up, stopped at the door, got out, and parking attendants would park their cars, and return them when they came out. I noticed that while this was commonplace at the high-profile establishments, there were relatively few places, particularly in the Santa Monica area, offering this service.

I decided to change that by starting a business with my brother called Pannonia Auto Parks. We concentrated on coastal communities, Santa Monica in particular. We quickly contracted to lease and run department store, restaurant, and hotel valet parking operations at places like the Miramar Hotel. The beach parking lots in Santa Monica were very lucrative, especially in the summer, and we could easily hire UCLA and Santa Monica City College students to park the cars.

We did well and my brother and I were soon driving Jaguars. He had a sedan, and I had a Jaguar XKE sports car. I also attained one of my great life goals by gaining my pilot's license and taking my first solo flight. I would eventually check out in Piper, Moony, Citabria, and Cessna aircraft, and flying would forever be one of my greatest thrills.

I learned the more money we made, the more desirable things we wanted to buy. I continued to get small parts in TV shows as well. It gave me a lot of pleasure when I was in a production that lasted a week or so, and the guards at the gate recognized me by the second or third day, even if it was just because of my car. Still, I wasn't making enough to produce a movie and fulfill my dream of really making it in Hollywood.

I had begun to realize that being a successful actor also meant being a successful businessman and decided to double my efforts on both fronts so I could reach all my goals.

To be closer to the majority of the parking lots we ran, my brother and I rented a house in Pacific Palisades on Linda Terrace. It was a two-story home on the corner of a cul-de-sac. The main floor was at street level, but because it was built on a slope, the second story was below the house. On a clear day, we could see the entire Santa Monica Bay.

It was a lovely area, and our neighbors were doctors, lawyers, well to do executives, as well as a lot of people employed in the movie industry. Pacific Palisades felt like a very peaceful little village tucked away in the Santa Monica Mountains and felt like a home away from home.

Our neighbors weren't as enthusiastic about having us on their quiet block as we were about being there. Here we were, a couple of apparent kids, and they thought we were up to no good. At best, we were disturbing their quiet neighborhood with our somewhat-loud parties. My neighbors to the south would not even acknowledge our existence.

At the time, I was a member of the American Institute of Fine Arts. This organization was basically a social club, which met monthly at different hotels around the greater Los Angeles area. I met and became friends with a lot of notable people there including the wife of silent film star Francis X. Bushman, General Doolittle, and Walter Braunschweiger, one of the founders of Bank of America

I decided to throw a party at my house and invited many friends, some from the Institute. I walked over to my neighbor who couldn't be bothered to return my friendly hellos over our shared fence. I introduced myself as if we'd just met for the first time and invited him and his wife to the party. It took a little salesmanship, but he finally agreed to come over.

Mr. and Mrs. Braunschweiger attended the party, as did some of the other notables like Iva Bushman. They were quite old at the time, so I sat them down in my living room on a prominent sofa. There were a number of people who knew them and made their way over to engage in conversation.

After a while, my neighbor asked who they were.

Glancing at the Braunschweigers who were sipping on some good Hungarian wine, I said, "Mr. Braunschweiger is the founder of Bank of America."

"Bank of America?" My neighbor almost dropped the glass in his hand. "How do you know them?"

"They are lovely people. Let me introduce you."

As it turned out, my neighbor was the general manager of four Bank of America branches in the Westwood and Beverly Hills Area.

Needless to say, he was very neighborly from that day on.

Iva Bushman called me one day and said, "John, would you like to meet a legend?"

"Of course," I said, without even asking who it was.

As it turned out. Mrs. Bushman was friends with the one and only Mae West.

Ms. West had invited us to lunch at her penthouse, which spanned the entire top floor of a high-rise in the old part of Hollywood. The décor was interesting, unusual, and luxurious. To me it was very old fashioned and reminiscent of the time of her fame.

Not only was she a huge star, but she was famous for having one or two muscle men in tuxedos in her movies as bodyguards in disguise. One of whom, coincidentally, had been Mr. Universe, Mickey Hargitay!

As we ate a delicious lunch served by Mae West's staff and engaged in lively conversation, I couldn't help but think about how my life had come full circle.

Steven and I grew Pannonia Auto Parks, moving on from restaurants and hotels to managing lots in high-rise buildings in Westwood, Beverly Hills, and the surrounding area.

A lot of actors including Don Rickles and Stephen Boyd lived in our buildings. When they came home, they'd pull up in front, and one of our valets would park their car in the garage below the building. When a resident wanted his or her car, they'd call down to our desk in the lobby and one of our attendants would bring it up for them.

In one of the high-rises, some residents wanted to park their own vehicles. It was very hard to do so because the parking stalls were smaller than normal size and it was hard to get in and out. Often, people hit the car next to theirs, causing damage. It was an issue that caused problems for us as well as the residents.

To solve this issue, I visualized, built, and eventually patented an accident prevention device I named the Automobile Parking

Accident Alarm System. Roughly described, I took strips of sponge rubber incorporating first and second electrical conductors and outfitted them with an aluminum shield and a mercury switch. We secured them to the rear walls, vertical columns, and even hung them from the ceiling in one of the garages. When these devices were engaged, even slightly, by a bumper or other part of an automobile, the conductors made electrical contact and an alarm would sound, deterring the driver from inadvertently scratching or denting their vehicle.

I sent my brother down to the Long Beach shipyards and bring a horn from a ship to connect to the system. He came back with what sounded like a foghorn. We hooked it up and tried it, but it was so loud down in the garage people as far away as the 12th floor were calling down to the desk to find out what was going on. Needless to say, I replaced the foghorn with something a lot less obtrusive.

We decided to exhibit our accident prevention device at a new product and invention show in LA. My brother built a model of a garage. He took four small toy automobiles and placed them in a cutaway section, installing our accident prevention device on the wall.

There was lots of interest but no buyer. On the last day of the three-day show, two men stopped by to find out if they could use it on a television show.

"Sure," I said.

"We want you to be on the show with us," they said.

"What is the show?"

"*You Can't Do That on Television,*" the man said handing me a card. "You'll gain great visibility for your invention."

Both my brother and I were at the studio at the appropriate time for rehearsal where they were going to feature a cutaway section of a garage and our little cars.

"We'll have a comedian asking questions all about woman drivers. You answer the funniest way you can."

"Don't worry, I am an actor," I said.

"You have a SAG card?"

"Yes," I said.

They both froze.

"What's the matter?" I asked.

"We can't do it now."

"Why?" I asked. It was the first time being an actor was going to keep me off TV.

"We would have to pay you because you are in the union."

"Let my brother do it. He's not a SAG member."

Steven was scared stiff, but he did the shtick and did it well.

Several million people saw the show. About a week later, we got a call from the 3M company wanting to see our invention. I agreed and sent them the patent pending explanation of my accident prevention device.

About two months later, I got a letter that said they'd had their engineers examine it and had decided not to get involved.

I'd hoped this would be my chance to make enough money to produce some kind of movie, but at least something I'd invented had made it to the small screen.

ACTOR'S STUDIO WEST

As a teenager in Hungary, the small theater where I performed was named after a man named Stanislavsky. At the time, I had no idea who Stanislavsky was, but, like everything else in those days, I didn't question it. We didn't have any right to question anything. Besides, everything had been renamed after Russians: streets, buildings, parks, and even cities.

Stanislavsky, as it turned out, had developed a technique and written a book called *An Actor Prepares*—a toolbox for actors to prepare themselves for the stage. Actors were encouraged to use experiences, memories, and object recall from their personal lives within their scenes. For example, theater actors are often called upon to cry, which is sometimes difficult to do. Stanislavsky used the example of an older actor whose son had been killed in a battle and was cremated afterwards. When a dramatic scene came up in the production, the actor would bring his son's urn onto the stage. When the time came for him to cry, he walked over to the urn, looked at it, and instantly shed tears. That sort of technique became known as Method Acting, or ultra-realism in acting.

At some point in the mid 1930s, the Moscow Art Theater Delegation came to New York where they performed a play utilizing this new Russian method. When it was time for the delegation to depart, a majority of the actors defected. They stayed in New York and propagated Stanislavsky's method. American actors joined them, and the Actors Studio New York was established.

When an actor named Lee Strasberg joined and became convinced that Method Acting was the only way to truly prepare for the stage, the Actors Studio became a secret society of sorts. To gain admission, actors performed three-to-five-minute scenes, which were critiqued by their fellow members and Strasberg himself. A lot of the big stars of the '50s, '60s and '70s were members.

Lee Strasberg eventually came west and set up shop in Hollywood, just below Sunset Boulevard in the donated old mansion of a silent film star. Part of the house became a rehearsal space and office. The garage became a small theater for the benefit of the members. Twice a year, actors could sign up to do a three-to-five-minute scene alone or with a partner. Afterward, there was a discussion where Lee Strasberg weighed in on whether the actor would be admitted. A lot of actors and actresses were not accepted even though they were already famous. There were stars who took the test several times and never gained acceptance.

The Actors Studio West existed for several years before I came to California, but I wasn't interested in exploring membership because of its Russian origins. However, one day, I read in the *Hollywood Reporter* the famously secretive and selective Lee Strasberg was going to hold a seminar at UCLA that would be open to the public. The response was so enormous, UCLA moved the seminar from a classroom to one of the largest movie houses in Westwood. Curious about what happened in the secret realm known as the Actors Studio, I decided to sign up.

I arrived in Westwood to a crowd of people. There were a lot of familiar faces in the audience, many of whom were recognizable actors. Staff from the Actors Studio made speeches and introductions. Then, Lee Strasberg himself appeared.

"I'm not here to teach but to give constructive criticism," he said.

Strasberg went on to say anyone who wanted to do a scene, either alone or with a partner, was to write their name, the scene they wanted to perform and its origins onto a piece of paper, and drop it into the large box in the lobby. Names would be drawn. Those asked to perform would do so with the minimal props provided. After the chosen scene, the actors were to stay on stage for critique.

I did not have a partner or scene prepared, and it wasn't as if they were offering a possible job or any help in getting work, but I decided to get up and see what was happening in the lobby.

While I was standing there, someone touched my arm.

"You're John, aren't you?" asked an aspiring actress whom I recognized from a casting call at one of the studios.

We chatted for a few minutes before she asked if I wanted to sign up and do something together. I was a bit hesitant but agreed to look for scenes that might work.

The next morning, we arrived at the seminar early and anxious. She had a list of possible scenes from plays and films.

"I have one picked out as well," I said. "A great scene that will run about five minutes and will be equally good for both of us."

"What is it from?" she asked.

"*The Seagull*, by Anton Chekov."

"The Russian play?"

"Yes," I said.

She agreed and we put our name and information into the box in the front lobby.

We began to rehearse that evening.

Each day at the end of the seminar, they announced the next day's victims. The next day, we all watched those actors perform and then endure critique exactly as it was done at the Actors Studio. Most of the time it wasn't a pretty sight.

My partner and I got called up two weeks into the seminar. We went on stage. I quickly arranged the set—if you could call it that—a bed, a couch, a small coffee table, and two chairs.

As I turned to face the audience—hundreds of actors waiting for us to fail (or so it seemed)—the scenario reminded me of my audition for acceptance into the Hungarian University of Film and Theater Art in Budapest.

I looked at my partner and heard Strasberg say, "Start."

We set up our positions on the narrow stage with the giant white film canvas behind us. Nervous, my scene partner mixed up her first line. Because of that, I became nervous and had to concentrate to help her out. In the fourth minute, I had to cry and hug her. Thankfully, I was able to shed real tears. Our performance ended and judgement day was upon us.

Strasberg started in and proceeded to tear my scene partner apart, questioning her about why she did certain things and telling her what she should have done. He brought up specific points and had no mercy for nearly forty-five minutes. I felt sorry for her, especially when she started to cry in earnest. I was also worried for myself. Had he saved the worst for last?

I kept waiting, wondering . . .

Weirdly though, Strasberg did not have one word of any kind for me.

I couldn't have been that bad, I thought. I actually wanted to hear assessment, or, rather, criticism from the man whose name was tied to so many successful thespians.

I got nothing.

Instead, I found myself consoling my partner by telling her Strasberg did not have the right to humiliate her like that. She went home that day wondering about her career in Hollywood. I wondered if I should even bother going to the next day's seminar.

Curious, I went anyway.

I was at the theater ten minutes before it started. There were still a lot of people in the lobby. Strasberg and his assistant were to one side, chatting. His assistant spotted me and waved me over.

"You did a good job yesterday. Mr. Strasberg and I want you to come to the Actors Studio and be one of us."

I could not believe what I was hearing. It was the equivalent of winning an Oscar.

To think, I almost hadn't shown up.

For months, I felt like an outsider at the Actors Studio West. Some of the other members behaved strangely towards me, and I couldn't figure out why. As it turned out, I was the only member invited without attending one of the official auditions that took place every six months. Of course, doing the scene with my partner in front of a large full movie theater was no small feat, but the regular members couldn't have known that.

Eventually, my anonymity faded and I became a full-fledged member of the secret society. People began to invite me to do scenes with them. I enjoyed the camaraderie and gained a lot of knowledge about acting. More than once, I thought about the fact that I would not have accepted the invitation had it been named Stanislavsky Studio West!

DETROIT WEST

I continued to get acting work, but I couldn't seem to get a permanent part on a series. In the meantime, my brother got married and moved with his new bride to another part of Los Angeles.

I was not satisfied with myself or with the trajectory of the parking lot business. Things just did not move fast enough for me. I had an idea though.

When we had a fender bender or scrape at one of our lots, we were often responsible for the repairs. As a result, I had developed connections to body shops around Santa Monica. It was a lucrative business, to say the least.

My brother and I discussed the situation and decided a career change was in order. We rented an old grocery store on Pico Boulevard and did extensive renovations until there was room for four cars in what had formerly been the cold storage area. We hired a professional body man with ten years' experience to work alongside my brother on the cars while I ran the business end and brought in work for the shop. The location was on a busy four-lane street, so we had visibility. I got to know the insurance companies who would refer customers with damaged cars.

Repair work rolled in from day one.

A few months after we opened our doors for business, a man came in accompanied by a boy in his late teens.

"This is Nabil. He is a Christian from Egypt who escaped his home country because of persecution. He doesn't speak English and couldn't find a job in New York, so he ended up here in California. I am trying to help him find a job that will make him enough to put food on his table."

His story was all too familiar.

"He has no trade, but he could clean up your shop and help your workers in some way."

I looked at this young man who was thin as a pole and knew I had to at least give him a chance. How many times had I been shown similar kindnesses? "I will give him a broom and have him keep the place clean. We will see how it goes from there."

The following day, Nabil came to work. He did a good job cleaning and was right there to help in whatever way we needed him. When payday came, we gave him his first check and went home for the weekend. On Monday, he came back and showed my brother the toolbox he'd bought with his money. Inside were a couple of shiny new tools. He kept on buying tools and continued helping with more and more of the work.

Nabil stayed with us for a decade. By then, we were a 35,000 square foot auto body shop with a mechanical department and two paint booths called Detroit West Auto Body & Paint. One of the most gratifying parts of our success was watching Nabil thrive. He learned English, brought over a wife from Egypt, bought a new car and a house, and had two great kids.

To this day, I am very proud we hired him!

ALL THE WORLD'S A STAGE

Due to war, the Occupation, and the Revolution, nearly 300,000 Hungarians lived in the greater Los Angeles area. I became a member of the Hungarian House. Headquartered on Washington Avenue in a historic 1910 mansion, they had a very active and professional theater group and a theater that could seat 100. Many former stars from Hungary had moved to Southern California thinking they could pick up where they left off, but had failed to consider the language barrier. Where some of these performers could draw a thousand people for three or four weeks at a theater in Budapest, here in the U.S. they were happy if they had a full house at a performance. As a result, many ended up making a living working as dishwashers at restaurants, house cleaners, and babysitters. Later on, a lot of them became realtors.

Nevertheless, the Hungarian theater forged on in Los Angeles. I performed in many productions despite some jealousy from the old pros—not because I was more talented, but because I'd been able to get on American television and had something of a chance to succeed where they could not.

I was cast as the male lead in a Hungarian House production about young love. Finding the female lead became a tricky matter because there wasn't an age-appropriate actress to play the part. Someone knew an architect in San Francisco with a younger sister who was visiting from Hungary. This lady had just graduated from the Film and Theater Arts University in Budapest, so they brought her to LA to see if she would be right for the part.

I was called into the Hungarian House to meet her.

As I walked in, I heard a beautiful piece from a Hungarian operetta and wondered who was playing. I could not see who was behind the upright piano. Not wanting to disturb the performance, I waited. Once the song was finished, I came around the piano to see the performer. She was beautiful, blond, and the right age for the play.

She was also right for me.

We were a hit together, on and off stage.

It was love at first sight. A brief courtship, marriage, and the birth of our beloved son Christian Deszo Czingula followed in short order.

My wife and I enjoyed celebrity status in the Hungarian community. When our son was born in 1971, all the older ladies in the Hungarian Community wanted to be his godmother, so we had to choose. The winner was the owner of the Hungarian newspaper in Los Angeles.

Christian, or Kristo as we called him, was a beautiful, gifted child. Before he could even walk, he would crawl on all fours out of the room, down the long hallway, and over to the piano where he would pull himself up by the bench. He would work around it until he reached the keyboard, and even though he was not tall enough to see the black and white keys, he would reach above his head and pound the piano. He definitely took after his mother and his Aunt Irén.

When Kristo was four, my wife and I were in a Hungarian play at the 1200 seat Wilshire Ebel Theater. The play started with a young child running across the stage to recite a single line and Kristo was perfect for the part. Most people in the audience knew who he was, and who his parents were, and he made us very proud by delivering his line perfectly. Performing on stage together was a true family highlight.

Unfortunately, his mother was uncomfortable about parenting from the start. She worried pregnancy might ruin her figure and, in turn, her career. Career was everything to her. I tried to help her succeed by making appointments with producers, directors, and agents, but she would turn up late for the appointment or come up with reasons why the role she was reading for wouldn't work. What she really wanted was to move back to Hungary where she knew she could establish herself at the level she desired.

There was no way I could return to Hungary permanently without the risk of persecution, nor would I allow my precious child to go back to Hungary and be brainwashed by Communism.

She was determined to go.

Five years in and our marriage was doomed.

At the time of our separation, we had a live-in South American housekeeper. My now-estranged wife took her and my son, and they all moved into an apartment in the San Fernando Valley without leaving a forwarding address.

Several agonizing months passed before I located them. My soon to be ex-wife was working long hours at a job in West Hollywood that barely covered rent. She did not make enough to pay her helper, who was watching our son. I paid the woman what she was owed, sent her on her way, and took over caring for Kristo—driving over there every night to put my young son to bed.

This went on for a month until the court granted me a divorce and sole custody.

Not long after, my son's mother returned to Hungary as a dual citizen and a parent who'd abandoned her responsibilities in order to pursue her dream of stardom.

My beloved son Kristo and I settled back into the Pacific Palisades house. We were inseparable from that point on. I hired a wonderful, loving older Hungarian lady named Margit Neni to live with us and help fill the void left by my son's mother.

Margit Neni had lived through a lot. Her Hungarian husband had come to the U.S during World War I, gotten a job at the Waldorf Astoria, and risen through the ranks to become the manager. He traveled back to Hungary in the 1920s and met Margit. They got married, and she came to the USA with him. Later, he managed the Fontainebleau hotel in Miami, Florida. They had a successful life and one daughter together, but by the time I met her, everything was gone, and she was living on social security.

She needed us, but we needed her more.

Kristo's life became pleasureful once again. He had his buddies in school and on the cul-de-sac. The elementary school was four blocks away. In the mornings, I would take him to school and Margit Neni would pick him up and they would walk home. She was wonderful and loved my son. Life had resumed a new semblance of normal.

Every year, the Hungarian newspaper sponsored a Hungarian ball. They asked me if I could contribute something to the entertainment. The ball was to be held at the Roosevelt Hotel in downtown Los Angeles and nine hundred people were expected.

I had met a nice young lady who was a member of the Kárpátok Hungarian folk-dance group, so I asked her for ideas; she suggested we do a solo dance number together.

"A folk dance?"

"No, no. As a matter of fact, I've got a great South American number we can use."

"Who would choreograph it?" I asked.

"You and me," she said.

I'd danced in public before but never as part of a performance like this. We practiced the dance we'd come up with and called in the lady who published the newspaper and was sponsoring the event to come take a look at *Fred and Ginger* in rehearsal. She loved it and decided we would do our performance on the main dance floor at intermission.

We performed our ten-minute number for the crowd dressed in authentic South American costumes. When it was over, we received an enthusiastic standing ovation.

Our joint venture also resulted in an affectionate friendship. Unfortunately, there were a couple of issues. Kristo didn't take to her. She was a brunette and he liked blondes, probably because of his mother. She was fifteen years younger than me and extremely jealous. My son was my first priority.

The romance fell apart.

I continued to parent with the help of Margit Neni.

FAMILY BUSINESS

In 1973, the oil crisis hit. People waited in lines four blocks long to fill their cars at the station where we bought our gas and oil for the shop. At one point, a driver pulled a gun on another motorist trying to cut in the line. No one wanted to buy big, gas guzzling American cars anymore, and small, economical Japanese cars began flooding the market. The whole economy suffered, but our auto body shop was hit particularly hard. We had to let workers go because we did not have enough work for them.

As a result, we decided to sell Detroit West. We knew the business itself wasn't going to bring a lot of money, but the property was worth ten times what we paid for it.

As a result of the sale, my brother and I had money—not enough for me to start a production company or for my brother who admitted he'd been dreaming about owning a white tablecloth restaurant—but we were able to take time off and travel. We were both American citizens, so we were able to get visas to go back for a three-week visit to Hungary. It was 1975, and neither of us had been back since we'd fled in 1956. We were both extremely excited to get back home after so many years.

Despite my passport and long-term citizenship, I was wrongfully detained briefly for being an enemy of the Hungarian people.

Thankfully, I was released quickly. We could hardly wait to get back to the good old USA but were so thankful to have been able to visit when my father Deszo Czingula passed away on April 8,1976.

Once we'd returned, I decided my best career path involved getting my real estate license. I learned that with a salesman's license I would have to work for a broker, so I decided to cut out the middleman. Once I had my broker's license, I signed up with a commercial real estate brokerage and sold a 24-unit apartment building within two weeks.

During that time, my brother was trying to put together his plan for a high-end restaurant and was realizing it wasn't as easy as he'd anticipated. I suggested he get into a hamburger or other food franchise, but he wasn't interested.

My successful apartment sale gave me an idea.

"Let's try to buy an apartment building," I suggested to Steven. "We'll fix it up, sell it, and use the profits to buy another one."

"How will that work?" he asked.

"You will organize a group of guys with the skills needed to rehab an apartment. I will search out a good buy. When I find something, you and your group jump on it, rehab it, and we sell it for a good profit."

"So, you want me to do all the work while you just make the deals?"

"At first it will be that way, but once you organize the work, which you'll understand after a couple of projects, your role will be to oversee and project manage. The faster a project is rehabbed, the faster we can put it on the market and make money. We'll keep doing that until we make enough so I can go into the movie business, and you can open your restaurant."

We agreed to give it a try and bought our first apartment building in Sherman Oaks. It wasn't a rehab, per se, but we got it for a very good price. I figured if we held onto it for a little while, we'd make a chunk of money. Close to the time of purchase, we had a vacancy. My brother, who'd recently divorced his first wife, promptly moved in saying, "Someone has to manage it."

He was only too glad to take on the role because there were a number of single ladies who lived in the building.

A few weeks later, I found a twenty-four unit apartment building in need of rehabbing. If we did the work quickly and cost effectively, we could make a lot of money. I had to borrow against the house in the Palisades, which I'd purchased several years earlier, so it was all the more urgent we finish the rehab in a timely manner. The project dragged on due to delays from the construction side. As a result, tensions began to increase between my brother and me.

Once we finally finished and sold it, I came across an excellent forty-unit apartment building at a very good price. It looked good from the outside and the interiors checked out as well.

We closed escrow.

Upon speaking with three tenants on the top floor, however, I began to hear multiple complaints about leaks. We had a professional inspection and learned the place needed a new roof. Judging by my brother's past performance, this project was just too much for him to organize and repair. Instead, I sold the building to a construction company for the same price I bought it. We did not lose money, but we did not make any either.

Though we'd experienced success with our valet parking business and the body shop, as well as a watch band and an optical business we'd launched, it was becoming clear our successful partnership was not ideal for this type of business. My idea of having one of us who excelled on the business and financing side and the other who'd play general contractor was not playing out quite how I'd hoped.

My old friend Dale called. "John," he said. "I have a little extra money, and I am going to invest in real estate."

"Great," I said. "Real estate is the best investment. I'll find you a deal and you won't have to pay me any commission."

"You don't have to do that," he said.

"I want to. The trip you organized to Mexico back in the day was epic and I still appreciate the 1940 Oldsmobile you found for me. It was my first car ever."

Dale was delighted.

A couple of weeks later I called him and said, "I found a fourplex in Sherman Oaks with four, two bedrooms, but all of them need a little work to get top rent."

We made a budget, including a very minimal down payment and necessary repairs. He went ahead with the deal, and it went into escrow. We decided to start renovations when he returned from a family vacation.

I discussed the project with my brother. It was a small job but needed to be done fast and under budget for my old friend. We got everything organized while he was gone.

Dale and his family returned, but there was a problem. He had not only spent all the money dedicated to the project, but had no idea how he was going to pay the bank for the loan payments. I never got a sufficient answer as to why.

My brother and I agreed the best thing we could do was make a deal with Dale and put the fourplex in our name. We would give him back the down payment he'd made, quickly fix it up, and resell the place.

We did just that, but my brother lost all enthusiasm for the business in the process. It took months and months for him to do the work and our relationship grew even more strained.

I learned two things from the experience; don't do business with friends, and while I loved my brother, our professional partnership needed to end.

EARTHQUAKE

By 1987, I'd transitioned from buying rehab properties and was working as a real estate broker. My brother had remarried, and we'd gone our separate ways businesswise. While I still loved the theater and acting, and had been more successful than many, it was time to focus only on ventures where I could control and grow my future. I continued to search and study businesses looking for something I could take on or create and make successful.

Los Angeles is a sprawling metropolis made up of sixty-plus smaller communities. Many of these communities had, or were in the process of creating, their own unique shopping areas or districts. Santa Monica had transformed a main street of already occupied, independently owned stores by redoing the sidewalks, planting more trees, building parking structures, and closing the street to vehicles so there was only pedestrian traffic.

I realized there were many communities that wanted a similar opportunity, so I created a business plan for a small shopping center called The Atrium that could be recreated in multiple smaller cities. For the maiden Atrium project, I decided to focus on my landing spot in Los Angeles—Whittier, California. The people who lived in Whittier were mostly executive types, and there was lots of money in this bedroom community. The main street was ideal for my plan, and the city was likely to respond positively to a customized shopping community.

I immediately put a down payment on two lots for sale in the middle of town, went to the city, and showed them my plan. My building would be the newest structure on the street with three stories, including escalators, elevators, and a glass roof. The ground level would feature three restaurants. I also planned to have a piano playing classical music in the lobby featuring players from the community. Right behind the two lots was the new city parking garage where customers could park for free. All they had to do was walk across from the three-story garage into The Atrium.

The city council approved it overwhelmingly.

By the time the architectural work was 70% complete, I already had about 30% of the place leased.

Then, tragedy struck in the form of the Whittier Narrows earthquake. Because the quake was centered directly below Whittier, almost every building on the street was damaged. The city parking structure was completely destroyed.

All of my pre-leased clients cancelled.

In thirty seconds, The Atrium idea had collapsed.

LIFE GOES ON

Career wise, I was licking my wounds. My personal life, however, took a turn for the better when I attended a Hungarian Christmas dance and met Ilona. She was blond, beautiful, and looked and sounded like Zsa Zsa Gabor.

Once again, I fell in love at first sight.

Even better, my new girlfriend and my son Christian got along beautifully. He was just finishing fourth grade, and he accepted her like she'd always been around.

We were married within months.

Life in the Palisades with my new wife and son was good. I spent many a Sunday sitting out on the porch, working my way through the *L.A Times*, and looking at the sailboats dotting the deep, blue Santa Monica Bay. The only thing that could possibly have made me happier was to have a boat of my own, which was to happen soon after.

My new wife was very artistically inclined. Beads and supplies from which she created beautiful necklaces, began to appear in the house,.

"You do lovely work," I told her, "but don't you already have more necklaces and bracelets than you can wear?"

"Yes, but I've been making them for friends too. One of my friends thinks I should sell them in the lobby of her high rise."

"I agree," I said.

Ilona began to make up designs and take them to her friend's condo complex on Saturdays where she'd gotten permission to set up a small table in the front lobby. In three hours' time, she would sell out of all her merchandise. She was very happy about her enterprise and began to sketch ideas for new designs—rings, broaches, bracelets, and more.

"Are you thinking of selling those, too?"

"Someday," she said.

"Who is going to make them?"

"Me. I want to learn how to make them."

"What are you thinking of making them out of?"

"Gold and semi-precious stones."

"And who is going to buy and pay for the material?"

"I was hoping you would help me," she said with a smile.

"It's an interesting idea, but I suggest you first learn how to make this stuff from silver and non-precious stones first." I liked the idea of starting a new enterprise because the real estate business had been slow, and I was getting tired of cold calling potential clients six hours a day.

"Or maybe I can have my designs made by some jewelry shop," she said.

"You could, but then that would make the product expensive to resell for a profit and you cannot claim you made it. You won't be able to make a name for yourself."

"You're right," she said.

"We have to find a trade school where they can teach you how to cut the image out of a silver sheet, and then how to hammer it into a certain shape, weld it, and polish it."

We found a jewelry-making school for Ilona and she enrolled.

I began to imagine a small jewelry manufacturing company, which could be grown nationally, and where my wife would be the star.

Before Ilona came along, I took my son all over—horseback riding on Catalina Island; motorcycle riding through the Santa Monica mountains; and even to mundane activities like business meetings. I wanted him by my side as much as possible.

As a result, Kristo had many interests. He wanted to be an actor. He also wanted to be everything from a policeman to a pilot, to a motorcycle racer, and swimming champion—the sports and adventure equivalent of the ambitious boy I had been.

We lived very close to the ocean and he had buddies who were surfers, so I bought him a surfboard. He was already a talented swimmer and quickly grew adept at surfing too. Unfortunately, there was a pecking order out in the water—the older surfers were always trying to scare away the younger kids to show them who was boss of the beach.

One Saturday, I got a call from the police. Kristo had been in an accident in the water and was on his way to the hospital via ambulance. Ilona and I jumped into the car and raced over. When we arrived, we were told he was in the operating room.

"The operating room?" I repeated, panicked out of my mind.

"You've got a very lucky boy here," the doctor told us. "Apparently, Christian was paddling toward a wave. One of the older boys was trying to scare him away and another got in too close. The waves were strong and took him even closer to your son. The older boy's back fin cut your son's neck open. It missed the main artery by a half inch. I've already cleaned the sand out of his wound and the scar will fade to nothing in time. He's going to be just fine."

"Do you know who did it?" I asked.

"You'll have to talk with the police, but I heard when the accident happened, the boy who hit him jumped off his surfboard, swam back out to fish Christian out of the water, and brought him on shore. I think he actually saved your son's life!"

While my son was recovering, we raced back to the beach and found a lot of people lingering there talking about the accident. I was determined to find out who had hurt my son, but no one knew who did it. My wife, who was infinitely more rational about the whole situation, agreed whoever had done it had also saved his life, and would have to live with the consequences of his bad behavior.

Thankfully, we brought Kristo home, alive and healthy.

Margit Neni was still with us in her apartment downstairs. She would come up to make breakfast when she knew my wife would still be in bed. Sometimes, I would spot her picking up a dish, turn around with it, and then stop to look at it for the longest time. This happened more and more frequently. I soon realized she had planned to use the dish she'd picked up but had forgotten why she'd gotten it in the first place.

It wasn't a good sign.

Kristo wanted to try his hand at acting, so I enrolled him at a place called Tree House Acting School for Children in Sherman Oaks. About three months in, we signed him up with an agent who specialized in child thespians.

Kristo went on to do several television commercials including 7-Eleven and GI Joe. He also did voiceovers. He was then cast as the grandson of a gangster gone straight in a TV series called *Scarecrow and Mrs. King*—a detective series starring Kate Jackson and Bruce Boxleitner.

I went to the studio to take Kristo to lunch to celebrate his new role. I was directed to a set of dressing room trailers with the actors' names written on the door. When I got to the third trailer and saw "Christian Czingula" written on the door of a 40-foot trailer, I was the proudest dad on the globe. We went out to lunch in the studio restaurant surrounded by actors who were also working on the lot.

The whole time, I had to fight the urge to point out my son and say to everyone, "That's my boy!"

All was well until Christian's agent sent him out on interview for another role and he was rejected because his voice had begun to change. The agent called us and said he couldn't send him for a while until his voice settled. Then, we would start again.

All along, I had wanted to enroll Kristo in a special Hungarian boarding school that was operated out of a castle in Bavaria, Germany. Run by a Hungarian organization, it was a school where children of Hungarian descent from all over the world learned about the language, history, and culture. I liked that they taught the old-fashioned way, like when I was a schoolboy in Hungary. I wanted my son to be part of the Hungarian community without all the Communist dogma. The program started in fifth grade. Given his voice was changing, the timing was perfect.

We flew to Germany and drove to the school, which was housed in a completely renovated thirteenth-century castle overlooking the mountains, just like in a children's storybook. Upon registration, a teacher took us to a room where Kristo would live with five roommates, all of whom were already there—two kids were from California, one was from Australia, one was from Spain, one was from Sweden, and one from England. I was amused all these kids spoke Hungarian but with different accents.

Curfew came and it was time for parents and guardians to leave.

We arrived back at the castle school overlooking the mountains in Bavaria to pick up Kristo for Christmas break. We were told at the office to find him in his room, at the gym, or down in the village near the school.

He wasn't in his room or at the gym.

As we walked down to the village, we walked by a gasthaus (tavern) and saw some teenagers coming out. I had a feeling Kristo was in there. Sure enough, he was seated inside with two other kids from school, drinking beer.

I was more than a little surprised and asked the bartender what was going on.

"In Germany, we are allowed to serve beer to students. We have an arrangement with them; they can only have a small glass called a piccolo. No more, and only on the weekend."

I didn't know whether I should be mad at my son or celebrate the small rite of passage that had already taken place. I was delighted, however, by the way the three kids were speaking to each other and to us in Hungarian.

Kristo was happy to hear we planned to take him on to Hungary to see relatives there during the break, but less so about finishing fifth grade at the Hungarian school. "We have to sit in our place, with our hands placed behind our backs. It's not like in America at all."

"That's the point," I said.

All the way to Debrecen, he grumbled he didn't want to go back.

The first time Christian went to Hungary, he was six years old and flew by himself under a special agreement with the airline in which they assigned one of the flight attendants to my son. She was responsible for him until she released him to my mother in Hungary.

This was a memorable trip for my son for many reasons. Back then, there was no refrigeration in Hungary. All the relatives and their kids were invited to my mother's house for dinner. Mother bought three live chickens at the farmer's market a few days in advance.

On the day of the big dinner, she proceeded to kill the chickens and let the blood flow out into a dish in front of my son.

As a boy, it had been my duty to kill the chicken for the family meal. My brother would help catch it, but I was the executioner. I hated doing it, but it also made me feel grown up to have that duty. I would take the chicken, hold the legs and the wings together, put her neck on a log, and chop her head off with my handy little axe. Then, I quickly let the blood flow into a deep bowl. The blood was always put into the hot chicken soup where it would cook and harden into a cake on the surface of the soup. Mother would divide it up among the family members saying it enriched our blood and made us healthy.

Kristo however, had no such life experience. He assumed that chicken meat came from the store wrapped in a cellophane package. He was horrified by the reality of what meat really was and never touched it again.

While he otherwise had an amazing time and looked forward to visiting again, my son had proved himself to be thoroughly American!

When the three of us arrived in Debrecen, we had a big, happy, family reunion at my younger sister's house. We reveled in this time together, especially with my mother who would pass away not long after, on August 31, 1981.

After several days, my sister got a phone call from my first wife, Kristo's mother. Somehow, she'd found out we were in Debrecen and wanted to take Christian for a couple of days.

"No," I said. "She can come here and see him, but she isn't taking him anywhere unless I accompany them."

"She is his mother," both my sisters said. "How can you be so cruel?"

All of my female relatives thought I was the devil for denying a mother the right to spend time with her child, but I feared she would take him out of the country and I'd never see him again. She was a dual citizen and could easily leave Hungary. I was called terrible, heartless, and more until I broke down and agreed to let my ex-wife have Kristo for two days.

She came and picked him up.

I was uneasy every second he was gone. Everyone told me I was being ridiculous. That was, until she didn't return at the appointed time.

I called the number she'd left, but no one answered. I waited all day, and they did not return. The next day, I went to the police.

I was despondent and didn't expect a big reaction. I figured the police wouldn't care much given he was with his mother. However, they went right into action and assured me they could keep her from leaving the country.

The next day, I got a call that my ex-wife and son had been spotted in a nearby town.

I got a car, and my wife and I rushed there. When we arrived, we were told they'd left but no one knew where. Unbeknownst to me, there was a national police search for them. She knew I would be looking for them, so she was constantly on the move.

The last location I was given was 200 kilometers away on the western side of the country. My wife and I took off and drove all day.

It was midnight when we reached the Danube. In the snow, fog, and darkness, we nearly missed the bridge we needed to cross. I was really worried my ex-wife was headed toward Austria. If she succeeded in getting out of the country, I would never see my son again.

I found the address, but they were not there.

I went to the local police and told them my story. The police captain assured me they would not be able to get out of the country. The border patrol had been alerted and were on the lookout. I had to appreciate how much the country had changed, at least in terms of the police since I'd made my own escape.

The police finally found them in a town not very far from the Austrian border, just as I'd feared. They gave us an address, which turned out to be an abandoned brick house. The police were already there when we arrived. The entrance to the building reminded me of a tunnel. I stood on one end of it with the authorities, and soon, to my enormous relief, my boy came running toward me.

We hugged each other tightly, both of us sobbing.

The whole episode reminded me of a Cold War-era spy drama where the Russians or East Germans and Americans exchanged prisoners over a bridge. I had no idea what happened to his mother, and I didn't care, only that my son was safe with me.

I notified the Hungarian school that Christian would not be coming back for the second semester. There was no imagining having him out of my sight like that again.

We spent another week in Hungary, and then returned to California where Kristo continued fifth grade at Paul Revere School in nearby Brentwood.

Even that was far enough away for me!

272

MUSIC AND JEWELRY

I asked my son what he missed most while he was in school in Europe.

"My piano," he said.

Everyone involved in his short Hollywood career said he had a good chance for success. And, of course, I was hoping to guide him with what I knew.

Kristo did not want to continue his acting career. He just wanted to play and write music.

At first, I was disappointed, but his talent would prove to be both bright and enduring.

I first realized how talented he was when we were on vacation at an all-inclusive resort in Jamaica. The meals, weather permitting, were always served outside between the hotel buildings and the beach. They also had a large stage with a ten-person orchestra playing at dinnertime. On Fridays, they had an amateur night. Guests with any kind of talent or interest in performing could sign up and were called onto the stage.

One evening, we heard the name *Christian Czingula*.

My wife and I sank down in our chairs, knowing our son had signed himself up. The musicians all looked a bit confused too when an unaccompanied eleven-year-old boy approached, took center stage, and waved the musicians over. He spoke to some of them and pointed to others. Everyone in the audience wondered what was going on and what was about to happen.

Kristo then walked to the microphone and introduced himself to the audience. "We are going to perform the song, '*We Are the World.*'"

With that, he walked up to the piano, signaled the musicians to start, and proceeded to play and sing the song, at times even directing the musicians. When the number was over, he took a bow and waved to the musicians to do the same.

The audience cheered and some even stood.

My wife and I were astonished, but even more proud.

"What did you tell the musicians when you called them over to the center of the stage?" I asked after we congratulated him.

"I just told them when they should come in as I was singing and playing the song. Don't you think it was nice that the audience started to sing along?"

We couldn't believe he'd had the courage and the know-how at his tender age. His stage presence must have come from the Tree House acting school. His interest in music had been apparent since he'd started crawling and was always at the piano. His talent came from both sides of the family— I liked to think I had a little something to do with it too.

Needless to say, my son Kristo, with the help of the orchestra, won first place at amateur night. The prize was a bottle of champagne. We ordered him ice cream since he couldn't drink, and the three of us enjoyed his winnings.

From that day forward, I called him Amadeus!

The boy's commitment to veganism was a bit more difficult to swallow. In sixth grade, he did a book report on *Diet for A New America*, written by John Robbins, the son of one of the founders of Baskin Robbins. In the book, the son criticizes how unhealthy ice cream is and goes on to explain in great detail the inhumane conditions inherent in the dairy and meat industries. Having witnessed his grandmother butcher chickens, the book only increased Kristo's zeal.

Kristo would not eat food cooked with or containing any sort of meat ingredients. For nearly two years, he insisted on being served an entirely separate meal from the rest of us. Finally, I put my foot down and said he needed to learn to cook what he wanted to eat.

I admired his commitment, but as a tried and true Hungarian omnivore, I can't say it was always easy.

Margit Neni was still with us but had increasing issues due to Alzheimer's. Her sister in Budapest wrote practically every week asking her to come back to Hungary and live with her. Margit was getting $500 dollars a month in Social Security, which her only daughter had talked the poor old lady into signing over. We all agreed it would be nice if Margit went back to Hungary to live with her sister, so we got her a lawyer to stop her daughter from cashing her checks. We were able to arrange for her social security money to be sent to Hungary. In those days, $500 American dollars was an enormous amount in Hungarian forints. The two sisters were able to live out the remainder of their lives in near luxury and go to restaurants, the theater, opera, and the zoo, practically every week. More important, when there was a complication with Margit Neni's health, her sister was there to help.

The plan took about six months to implement. When we took Margit to the airport, we all cried because she had become a part of our family. We missed her immediately, but we knew this arrangement was best for both her and her sister.

After Margit Neni's departure, I began to notice Kristo was spending a great deal of time downstairs in what were her rooms. Two weeks passed before he appeared in the living room and stood in front of me like he always did when he wanted to negotiate something. I pretended not to notice and continued to read my newspaper, knowing he would rustle the edge of the paper when he was ready to say whatever was on his mind.

"I have an idea," he finally said.

"If you want a moped, it's non-negotiable." For years the biggest arguments my son and I had had were over his desire for a moped. The traffic on Sunset Boulevard from our house to school was very dangerous and I simply wouldn't allow him to put himself in harm's way on that famously twisty stretch of road.

"I have a better idea and you will like it," he said.

"Which is?"

"I want to build a studio downstairs."

"A recording studio?"

"A music studio. I want to form a band with some friends from school and we need to get together and practice."

I was reminded of the time when he was in elementary school and I'd hired a retired opera singer to teach him piano. She instructed him to play the scales because it was the best way to learn, exercise his fingers, and practice. After three lessons she came to me and said, "I am sorry, but you're wasting your money with me. He doesn't want to learn, and I don't think he has talent for the piano."

When I asked Kristo what the problem was, he said, "I thought she would teach me songs. I want to play jazz, reggae, and rock and roll. I don't need to play the scales all day. I already know how to play the piano. I want to learn songs."

"How exactly do you build a studio?" I asked, wondering how far this would actually go.

"Well, we first have to soundproof it because the neighbors will be all over us if we don't. I already have that covered though."

"And how's that?"

"Egg cartons are the best for soundproofing and I have already talked to a few restaurants and grocery stores. They've agreed to save them for me instead of throwing them out. I will also do the rest of the work involved. I just might need some money."

Kristo collected so many egg cartons I had to tell him to use the ones he had and to only get more when and if he needed them. I only helped my son work on his studio when he asked for help. I wanted him to learn there was a difference between a good idea and what it actually took to make it happen—the work and discipline. I did, however, provide him a bit of capital.

Kristo had his fellow musician friends over to discuss how they were going to proceed. His gatherings also served as something of a test. He wasn't just having friends over to have a good time jamming but seemed to be assessing their qualifications for his band.

Once the room was done, he placed his electric piano so he could see all the other instruments. The drummer arrived with his equipment that first weekend. The rest of the boys brought various pieces of equipment as they showed up for rehearsal.

A complaint about the drum noise came in after the very first rehearsal. As promised, my son talked to everyone within earshot of the house. The consensus was the best time to rehearse would be from 11:00 a.m. to 3:00 p.m. on Saturdays.

I welcomed everything about this musical gathering at my house. I knew exactly where my son was and what he was doing. By the time Kristo became a high school student, the studio had become a place where the kids came to jam. The drug situation was bad amongst teenagers at that time and I was not only happy my son had found a positive creative outlet where he wanted to be during his free time, but had been industrious enough to create it and run it himself.

Kristo continued to be serious enough about music to actually make a career out of it, but while he was young, there was always an ever-changing group of teenagers having fun and playing good music.

In the meantime, my wife's jewelry-making enterprise was also progressing. She attended two-week intensive classes, which focused on different aspects of the jewelry-making process. It was expensive, but I was happy to see all the effort she was putting in.

She would acquire a large sheet of silver, cut out the rough shape of the item, for example, a broach, and then start to shape it with her newly acquired knowledge. After a few months of this, the house, in particular the living room, became a "shop" filled with silver pieces, sheets, tools, beads, and assorted supplies. She still wanted to make her designs out of gold and semi-precious and precious stones.

"I need an electric-buffing apparatus," she said one day.

"I think we should go down to Santa Monica and find workspace to rent," I said. "But first, you should go around to some of the retail stores and test the market for your beautiful stuff. What you are doing is no longer a hobby, it's becoming a business."

"What are we going to call the company?" she said, agreeing with me, at least in theory.

"How about Ilona C. Designs?"

"I like it, but what is the "C" for?"

"It's your first name and the C is me, the financier."

"But . . ."

"But what?" I asked.

"Oh, nothing. I like it. It sounds good," she said.

I should have questioned her more. Instead, I said, "Let's make up a brochure with pictures of your products and some information about you so you can make a run at this. At least enough to make back what it's cost so far. We'll test this out, and if you make sales, we'll launch Ilona C. Designs."

Once we had the brochure and business cards made up, Ilona put on her best dress and her Hedda Hopper hat and went straight to Beverly Hills with samples.

Lo and behold she got a trial order for some of her pieces.

"Let's think about the equipment you would need for a shop," I said.

"I'll also need workers."

"We'll hire help as needed. Paying for rent and materials is already a large expense."

My wife began to pursue more department stores to carry her silver designs. Despite the appealing design and wholesale price points, department stores did not pan out as a viable retail option because they did not sell enough product. I began searching around the television market, hoping to find a way to get her jewelry onto a home shopping TV show. I located a family-owned closed-circuit television company in San Diego.

It turned out they were operating twelve hours a day, seven days a week, selling small household items like small furniture, dishes, and jewelry. An on-air hostess held the merchandise up to the camera and explained all the details of the product. The at-home audience could ask questions. If someone asked her to move or turn the product and show another side of it, she could. In other words, the member customers could communicate in real time with the presenter. They had 40,000 customers in San Diego alone and owned two other stations, one in Oklahoma, and one in Texas.

We drove down to San Diego and showed them our merchandise.

The station manager agreed to try out the silver jewelry.

I also had an idea to jazz things up—since my blond wife looked a little and sounded a lot like the Hungarian Hollywood star Zsa Zsa Gabor, I asked the station manager to let her sit on the stage in front of the camera when Ilona C. Designs were scheduled to be shown on the program. She and the presenter could discuss the merchandise together with the call-in customers.

They agreed.

Ilona took to the stage with the regular presenter, and they had a great time talking jewelry. It was a hit! So much so that my wife started to get fan letters from the audience! In addition, management began to ask her to expand her offerings.

"They asked me if I have a design for ladies' watches," she said one day.

"What did you say?" I asked.

"I am working on it."

I actually did the leg work and found out ladies' watches generally came in three sizes. While the bulk of the interior mechanics were produced in Japan, the watches themselves were assembled in Hong Kong. All we had to worry about was the design, which was basically the case for the inner mechanism. I got the name of a respected manufacturer and bought us two round trip tickets to Hong Kong.

When we got there, we were surprised many of the skyscrapers in Hong Kong were actually factories. Some even had elevators designed to carry a big truck inside.

We had an appointment in just such a building with a watch manufacturer. We met with them in a small office and told them exactly what we wanted in a ladies' watch. Then we toured the small workspace where nearly thirty workers sat shoulder to shoulder at tables putting the Japanese interior mechanics into watch cases.

My wife picked out about a dozen case models and asked if she could make some changes by drawing her designs on a piece of paper. The manager asked us to come back at 11:00 a.m. the next day.

When we returned, the designs she'd created had been produced and were ready for us to look at. They were very impressive and well-priced. We could now say they were created by Ilona C. Designs.

We put in a trial order, paid for it, and away we went sightseeing in Hong Kong. About five days after our return, the package from Hong Kong was in our hands at Ilona C. Designs in Santa Monica, California.

Incredible efficiency!

We traveled extensively as a family and enjoyed family time at my timeshare in Moorea, Tahiti. Ilona also urged me to invest in a timeshare in Lake Tahoe. She thought we would use them to invite and entertain business clients in both real estate and the jewelry business. Although it never really evolved that way, we enjoyed the three-bedroom property for both world-class winter skiing and stunning summer getaways. One of my best memories from Tahoe was winning a thousand dollars cash, not in one of the casinos, but via lottery ticket. Kristo and my wife encouraged me to buy a scratcher ticket at the local grocery store. Kristo scratched it out right at the cash register. We actually won the top prize—$1000.

Kristo was a junior in high school when we got an invitation to attend the Palisades High School music festival. After speeches and introductions by various teachers and students, the orchestra performed and did an excellent job. After intermission, the teacher announced the jazz band, featuring Kristo on the piano and as leader of the band. Kristo loved to play jazz and the performance was a great success. There was clapping, cheering, and people dancing in the audience.

Afterward, we spotted the music teacher. We congratulated him on his fine work with the students and introduced ourselves as Christian's parents.

"Christian is a very talented musician," he said. "Especially on the piano."

"What do you mean, especially?"

"He can play just about any of the instruments in jazz band."

We had no idea.

"He is going to go a long way in the music business. I suggest you look into a college like Julliard in New York. He has what it takes."

I felt very proud of my son.

With the teacher's encouragement, we had a lot of discussions about applying to Julliard and how an education of that caliber positions a musician for his or her career. Julliard was also known for its drama program, and I still had high hopes for him, now on both fronts.

"Not interested," Christian said every time I broached the subject. "I create my own music, and I don't want anybody to ruin my work."

He enrolled at Santa Monica College instead.

The American Institute of Film Arts was hosting an event to honor the late Lauritz Melchior, a famous baritone and a member of the Metropolitan Opera. His son, a movie producer in his mid-60s, would attend the luncheon and accept the honors.

The president of the organization knew Christian played piano and asked if he would play a classical piece as entertainment. I figured it would be a bit tricky to convince him, but Kristo loved to perform and had nearly ten days to learn a classical piece.

At first, he refused. He only played jazz and reggae and didn't want to learn *anyone else's* music.

Needless to say, I began to pull my hair out.

The day before the luncheon he finally agreed to perform, but only if he could write the classical piece himself.

Oh, boy, I thought, and began to hold my breath.

The luncheon was on a Sunday. On Saturday, at about noon, Kristo began to work on his piece. We heard him tinkering on the keyboard all day but hadn't heard the complete piece.

Late that evening he finally said, "I have written something. Do you want to hear it?"

We didn't know what to expect, and I was concerned he was going to embarrass himself badly in front of this distinguished group.

I was completely wrong. The piece was excellent—ten minutes long and sounded like something France Liszt might have written. Not only was it beautiful, but entirely presentable to any connoisseur of classical music. While it took an hour to talk him into it, Christian even agreed to put on his navy-blue suit, white shirt, and a tie for the performance. He hadn't done that since his graduation from high school two years earlier.

When we arrived at the hotel there were about seventy-five people, all 65 or older. I knew we had the right music to honor Lauritz Melchior.

"Play with vigor," I told Kristo just before he sat down in front of the grand piano. "You have long, bold hair, so throw your head back at the appropriate times. And, if you want, break a few black keys dragging your hands across them like Franz Liszt used to do. Don't worry. I'll pay for the broken keys."

All the guests were served lunch. There was a speech about the life and career of Lauritz Melchior. Finally, the president of the American Institute of Fine Arts introduced my son by saying he'd seen Christian for the first time as a four-year-old stage actor at the Wilshire Ebel theater. He also told the audience my son had been a child actor in a lot of commercials and TV shows, but he had turned to music and would play his own composition in honor of Lauritz Melchior.

Kristo did all the physical moves and expressions exactly as I'd asked him. Although he did not go as far as to break any black keys, his performance was wonderful and the audience loved him. Not only did they clap thunderously, he got standing ovations—especially from the older ladies in the crowd. Lauritz Melchior's son shook his hand and congratulated him heartily.

I could tell none of this meant much to Kristo.

"They really liked you and your composition," I said.

"It's not my music," he simply said in response.

At that moment, I recognized the same nonchalance of his biological mother. Kristo had put on his first and last classical music performance that day. Little did I know, this would be our last outing together as a family as well.

COMMUNICATION BREAKDOWN

The jewelry business was still going, but our only retail sales outlet was the closed-circuit TV station. By this time, Kristo was attending Santa Monica College and talked more and more about vegetarianism and Buddhism. I figured he was trying to exert his independence and his entry into adulthood, but we spoke less and less. We couldn't even have a conversation about acting or even music. He still played the upright piano in the living room constantly.

My wife and I did not communicate very well either. I'd brought her younger brother to the United States and gotten him a job where he could learn a whole new trade as an architectural model maker. He lived with us for some time, and I hoped that would make her happy. He and Kristo got along well. They called each other "Big Foot." Having him around didn't lighten the general mood though, and my wife and I argued far too frequently. Given my real estate brokerage business was slow, the sun wasn't shining much at all upon our family.

When the TV company announced to us they were negotiating to sell their business to a national company, it put the future of Ilona C. Designs into question. The news just added to our family stagnation.

I encouraged my wife to talk with the national company purchasing the San Diego outfit to see if they would be interested in carrying and selling Ilona C. merchandise. They agreed to meet with us, and we engaged in promising negotiations. The sticking point was they wanted us to have $1,200,000 worth of our products in their warehouse six weeks in advance of each show in which our products would be featured. That meant we had to produce and stock over a million dollars worth of inventory at all times. Depending on the sales flow, that could mean an output of as much as $6,360,000 per year to have inventory at the ready. We would have to ramp up production, employ more workers, and buy a lot more materials. The big kicker was if the merchandise didn't sell, we had to agree to take it all back.

We had no other accounts of substance and there was no way we could front all that expense, so I told my wife we needed to close down Ilona C. Designs, LLC. She was understandably upset, but she was also oddly nervous.

As I was going through paperwork, I noticed the business was registered in her name only. My name had never been put on any document as an owner or partner. When I told the young Hungarian couple we employed at the shop we were closing and had to let them go, they told me in confidence that my wife borrowed $20,000 from them. I could not believe my ears. She'd borrowed money from this new immigrant couple without my knowledge? They were shocked she'd never mentioned the loan to me.

I surmised my wife had imagined the company bearing her name would grow, she'd make a name for herself as a designer, and then divorce me. Because the business was in her name, her plan was that she'd get everything.

At the beginning of our life together, Ilona wanted to get remarried every five years to prove, how much we loved each other. We'd spent nearly ten happy years enjoying each other's company and traveling together to Hungary, Hawaii, the South Pacific Islands, and Jamaica. She was my son's stepmother and my companion.

I remember when a friend of mine got married. Six months later, his wife divorced him and tried to take away the house he'd owned for years before he met his wife. She also wanted an outrageous amount of money in spousal support. My wife was totally outraged. "How can she do this to the poor man?" she asked and swore she could never do anything like that.

When Ilona and I separated and filed for divorce, she wanted the jewelry business and all the equipment associated with it. The young couple who worked for the jewelry company wanted to go back to Hungary because the wife was expecting. I told them I'd be in Hungary soon and I'd call them and arrange to pay back the entire amount in U.S. dollars.

When I got to Hungary, I called them in Budapest and asked them to come to the American Embassy. The husband showed up, and we went into the Embassy together so we could have a witness to the exchange of money and the receipt process. After our transaction, he told me his wife was due to have their baby soon and they'd inherited a small house. They planned to use the money to fix the house up in preparation for the baby and to start a vegetable garden.

It felt good to know I'd been able to repay their money on my soon to be ex-wife's behalf, and that they trusted me.

The divorce went smoothly because I gave Ilona everything she wanted and paid her lawyer's fees. Just for good measure, I gave her the Moorea and Lake Tahoe timeshare contracts which I'd almost paid up. She was ostensibly satisfied and about to make her mark on the world as a jewelry designer.

Apparently, things didn't go according to her plan because a few years later, I heard she was working in a department store as a jewelry sales clerk.

During this time, Christian moved to Venice, California. Soon after, one of his buddies invited him to go to Hawaii for the summer. The young man's father, a financial adviser, had a big house there where they could live. So, off Kristo went.

While he lived in Hawaii, he sowed his oats and worked in an outdoor market selling trinkets to tourists. Eventually, he met a girl and they fell in love. She wanted to stay in Hawaii with him, but her parents wouldn't hear of it. They were young and in love, so she borrowed money and flew back to Hawaii to be with my son. They lived together for a time, eloped, and returned to live in her hometown, Friday Harbor, Washington.

Their early life together included the purchase of a forty-foot school bus to rebuild into an RV. They planned to make recordings of the music he wrote and travel the country, playing concerts, and stopping at all the radio stations along the way in what they envisioned as a grassroots campaign to get his songs on the air. Ultimately, they planned to catch the attention of a record company and get him signed to a record deal.

"If Elvis Presley could do it," Kristo said, "so can I."

I told him the music business didn't work like that anymore. Besides, they didn't even have the money to convert the bus into an RV.

To help them out, I paid for the materials and his father-in-law, a retired sheriff and a very good carpenter, helped with the renovations. By the time it was finished, they had a living room, kitchen, full size bathroom, and a bedroom created by cutting a VW Bus in half horizontally and welding it to the top of the school bus. That left plenty of room for a music studio inside—electric piano and the whole nine yards.

Christian and his wife traveled across the country as planned and ended up in Florida. Needless to say, his original idea of becoming a rock star did not materialize. However, my son did get gigs in beach hotels and restaurants performing his original music.

When his wife got pregnant with twins, they returned to Friday Harbor and then moved back to the Big Island of Hawaii so the babies would be born there.

I flew to Hawaii in 2002 when the babies, Eden and Lili, were three days old. I had always wanted daughters and called them my Hula Girls. They were beautiful, and have grown up to be artistically talented, but one of the babies had some physical challenges to overcome, so they moved back to Friday Harbor so they could be near family and get the extra support they needed.

Unfortunately, it was difficult for my son to do anything musically in Friday Harbor, and it took its toll on the marriage. He and his wife divorced when the girls were five years old. He moved back to Florida and has been able to play music under contracts he has secured at various resorts. He also started what has become a successful DJ business.

ALL BUSINESS

I was divorced, my son was grown and a father in his own right, and my time was my own. I missed my son and my wife, but I had taken the marriage test and failed twice. I needed to accept my weaknesses and focus on my strengths. I decided to direct my attentions toward business. During all the years I'd been supporting my family and funding their entrepreneurial ventures, I'd been thinking up inventions and businesses of my own. Now free of entanglements—financial and otherwise—I was ready to make my entrepreneurial mark once again.

My first invention, an electronic emitting device, was the logical extension of the first crash prevention system I designed. This creation—a sensor to avoid car crashes—turned out to be well ahead of its time. In my plan, cars could be outfitted with an electronic signal the car ahead of it would receive via a sensor on its bumper. This interaction between cars would control the speed of the car and the distance between the two cars so they would not collide.

While the idea was well-received, implementation was cost-prohibitive. Because of its use in automobiles, the system needed NTSB approval. Transportation laws would have to be changed, and the government would have had to force automobile manufacturers to build new cars equipped with the system. In addition, the necessary computer technology to make it financially viable was still years away. In other words, the cost to implement what was a relatively simple system quickly rose into the billions.

Every time I mentioned my new idea, people were ready to put me in a straightjacket. "You're crazy," they said. "That's not possible."

Thanks to Elon Musk and some brilliant advances in computer technology, my idea comes standard in most cars made today.

I started and ran a company for ten years called Univer Foods through which I imported food items like paprika and garlic paste from Hungary, and which I sold to wholesalers. As part of this venture, I wrote a cookbook entitled *For the Love of Paprika*, which was published by ÉdenLili Publishing Company.

Simultaneously, I developed a national marketplace concept called Gourmet Cookery Marketplaces. My idea was to create a free-standing store or area within a store where the general public could purchase menu/recipe-based groceries using computerization, automation, electronic video, and internet technologies. I put in a patent application for this method of retailing which featured pre-selected raw gourmet ingredients to be cooked by customers at home. The Gourmet Cookery Marketplace was designed to save time, energy, and money because customers would be able to pick meals from hundreds of different dishes and order via time-saving methods such as the internet, telephone, and fax. I also envisioned cooking demos, a test kitchen facility, a television cooking show, and a magazine.

I had meetings with several different grocery store chains about devoting a section of their stores to the Gourmet Cookery Marketplace concept, but it proved to be cost prohibitive.

These days, meal kit delivery—a logical offshoot—is popular and commonplace.

No matter what business I was pursuing, my father's idea— to harness the heat from underground thermal springs to build our greenhouses—stuck with me for its simple brilliance and kept me thinking about alternative energy.

As a teenager, I thought about alternate uses for the movie houses in Debrecen. They stood locked all day until four o'clock in the afternoon when they opened for the public. In those days, I tried to imagine a mechanical way the rows of seats could be lifted from the floor so water could be sprayed in and quickly frozen, so people could come and ice skate during the day. It was fantasy, of course, but using structures for multiple purposes made perfect sense to me.

During the first oil crisis of 1975, I began to think seriously about how the rays of the sun could be used to produce energy and became fascinated by the possibilities inherent in solar energy. I rarely discussed the idea with my family because I knew they wouldn't understand or support my interest in such an unheard of technology. The idea continually nagged at me for years.

On the way home from one of my yearly visits to Hungary, as we were landing at LAX, I looked out the airplane window at a vast vista of warehouse rooftops—hundreds of thousands of square feet with nothing but air conditioning equipment on top. I began to wonder if there was a way to utilize that space to create steam power that could be turned into electricity, not only for the buildings themselves but that could be sold to the power companies. At the time, solar power was the newest frontier. I wanted to take it further and make steam from the sun to turn a turbine, which would create electricity like they did with oil, gas, and coal. It was bigger, crazier, and had more potential than any business idea or invention I'd ever thought up.

In the spring of 1991, I decided I would dedicate my life to making it happen.

STEAM FROM THE SUN

For the next seventeen years, all my efforts revolved and evolved around my quest to create steam from the sun—turning theoretical fantasy into reality.

I spent the first five years experimenting with solar high-temperature technology, working to accumulate the money and brainpower I needed to make my concept a reality.

Warehouses in general are poorly constructed, particularly the roof areas. My solar concept involved a lot of water and I was concerned most large rooftops couldn't withstand the weight of the equipment, much less the water. To solve this issue, I partnered with a contractor in Medford, Oregon and we began to work together on how we might retrofit existing structures to accommodate the weight of such an invention.

Because I was still working in real estate, I met a developer who had plans for a huge resort in Palm Springs, which had a golf course, hotel, restaurants, and swimming pools. He gave an informational dinner for potential investors in a private room at a hotel in Santa Monica. At that dinner, there was a contractor present from North

Carolina whose company he planned to hire for the build-out. The magnitude of this project was enormous, but the real estate market was very weak at the time. In addition, Palm Springs had more than enough existing resorts and golf courses. I left without making any commitment to get involved, figuring I'd wait and see how it evolved.

The developer called me a few days later and asked me to invest in another venture: office buildings in Denver, Colorado. One was a freestanding 72,000 square-foot single-story office building with a 680 space parking lot near I-70. The other properties were two fairly new four and five-story office buildings on Parker Road. He said he had large down payments on all three properties and was interested in having me partner with him.

I agreed to go view the properties. The real estate market was very sluggish in Colorado at that time, and I could tell he'd gotten in over his head and was looking for my money to buy himself time to attract bigger investors.

I flew to Denver to look at the properties. I had no interest in the office buildings, which were practically empty because the economy wasn't there to support them and the price was high. The 72,000 square foot one-story office building, however, was a very nice property. It sat on five acres of land, had a 640 car parking lot across the street, and was located just a block from I-70—close to where the new airport was going in. The only downside was it was a one-tenant building. Even then, it could be rented out in parts to different commercial companies.

I decided to speak with the owners—an insurance company who'd built the building for themselves. I learned they were selling because the location didn't suit them, and they wanted to relocate to a high-rise near downtown.

I called the real estate developer to give him my thoughts, but before I could say anything, he said, "John, I'm sorry I had you fly all the way out there because I am having some unexpected financial and personal issues. I'm going to have to cancel my involvement in the two office buildings entirely."

"What about the single story on I-70?"

"I don't have any paperwork signed yet. I met with them a couple of times, but there is no contract of any kind."

The conversation was abrupt and I needed to regroup, so I went to a nearby McDonald's and had a hamburger and a Coke. When I was done eating, I went back to the one-story building and walked around it a couple of times. I wasn't interested in the two office buildings at all, but this was an interesting property.

I went back inside, sat down with the vice president in charge of handling their real estate, and negotiated a deal to buy the building for $1,100,000 with a down payment of $210,000 and no payments for a year and a half. During that time, I figured I would be able to refinance with a bank or other financial institution. In addition, they gave me $25,000 dollars to clean up the property.

As soon as the title to the building was in my name, I called CB Commercial Brokers, listed the property with them, and went back to Pacific Palisades.

I had become a million dollar commercial property owner with a property worth twice as much I'd paid for it.

I contacted my partner in Medford, Oregon and told him it was time to get serious about Solar Power International. We'd toyed around with all sorts of contraptions designed to make steam from the sun, but none of them worked. Now that I owned a significant piece of real estate that could potentially be used to attract investors to Solar Power International (as I'd named my company), I felt like it was time to put all of my attention toward the project.

I began to drive back and forth from Los Angeles to Medford on a weekly basis so we could try out various inventions. The most promising was a large box with a type of magnifying lens on top made by attaching multiple lenses together to form a square lens. The idea was that when the sun shone on the lenses, water stored underneath would turn into steam.

It didn't work.

We also built a contraption in which we bought some eight foot, aluminum sheets and made a curvature with a big surface area by connecting three of them together, side by side. We attached this large panel to a frame and a bicycle chain so we could turn it on its axle toward the sun. Once in a while, we heard quick buzzing noises from the panels and couldn't figure out why. Upon investigation, we realized tiny bugs would fly into the concentrated sun rays and burn up instantly.

It didn't work either.

Creative as we were, we needed the additional brainpower from engineers who could actually design a workable apparatus. The internet and computer search engines did not yet exist as we know them today, so I got on the telephone and started to cold call (a skill I'd learned as a real estate broker) engineering firms.

I couldn't find anybody who took my questions seriously.

My weekly drives from Los Angeles to Medford on the 5 Freeway took me along the California Aqueduct, which came from close to San Francisco and flowed south to LA, providing precious water to all the farms along the way. Not to mention millions of people in Southern California.

Which also got me thinking . . .

After five months of back and forth, including more than a few detours to observe the aqueduct at different points along the route, I decided to make a stop in Sacramento at the agency managing the California Aqueduct. Much like I did when I first wanted to be an actor or was interested in getting my ex-wife's jewelry on television, I went right in and asked the receptionist to speak to someone.

Finally, an engineer came out and greeted me.

"I drive alongside the aqueduct twice a week on my way to and from Los Angeles, and I've grown curious. I am very interested in solar technology, and I've wondered why it is not covered. It flows nearly 700 miles in the California sun, so you must lose a lot of the water to evaporation.

"Close to half by the time it gets to LA," he confirmed.

"So why isn't it covered?"

"It was built by the Army Corps of Engineers in the early 1940s. Back in those days they considered it too expensive," he said. I could tell he appreciated my question though. "We have a book that tells you all the data you want to know about the aqueduct if you'd like one."

He returned with a little blue book, which I studied backward and forward. From then on, I stopped into the California Aqueduct office regularly. I also had my favorite spots to stop, rest, and study the man-made river. According to the little blue book, it was a standard hundred feet wide. It was so well-designed one could hardly see the water flowing. There were ripples only when the wind was blowing strong. Yet, if something fell in, it was swept downriver quickly. I also realized even though it had concrete sides and bottom, there had to be sediment collecting, namely dust, which would settle and become mud. The Army Corps of Engineers had compensated for that by creating a specially designed cleaning machine which was utilized from time to time to clean the bottom completely.

I came up with what I knew to be a good idea—if the aqueduct could be covered with traditional solar panels, it would conserve water, alleviate the need for the periodic cleanings, and even make money.

I didn't want to be told I was crazy, because I'd heard that far too often, so I didn't share my idea, but by stopping at the offices, I got to know about six or seven of the engineers. One of them theorized, "We figure you are writing a book about the aqueduct, so if you do, just remember to spell my name right!"

Another even said, "I think you want to cover the aqueduct to save the water that evaporates on the way to LA. That would be a good idea."

We applied for and eventually received a patent to cover all 750 miles of the California Aqueduct with solar panel technology.

I kept cold-calling in the hopes I might find an interested engineer or investor for SPI but with no luck.

One day, close to a year after I started driving to Oregon and back, I happened to think about the contractor who'd come to Santa Monica to meet with my developer friend about his Palm Springs project. I remembered from that meeting he was the CEO of a 106-year-old construction company in North Carolina. He had impressed me with knowledge and success.

It took me two days to track down the company name and get my courage up to give the man a ring out of the blue.

"What can I do for you?" he asked when we got down to business.

"I thought I'd call you and tell you about an interesting idea."

"Which is?"

"As you are probably aware, everyone is talking about solar power as the energy source of the future. Even the government is offering financial help to startups."

"Interesting subject, the solar business," he said. "We do a lot of work with an architectural firm called Innovative Designs. They are specialists who only get involved with designs that include alternative energy."

It felt like the first true nibble on my line.

"I'm hoping you might be interested in investing or participating in a solar energy business a step beyond the current technology of installing little blue panels on rooftops," I said.

"As in?"

"We will be making steam, capturing the steam, and turning a turbine to make electricity."

"From the sun?"

"Exactly."

"Isn't that aiming a little high?"

"Not as far as I am concerned. We plan to pioneer this technology."

"And you need financial help to make that technology successful?"

"Yes, but also brainpower."

"Where is your company located?"

"Right now, Solar Power International is in two places. I am in the L.A area. My partner is a contractor in Medford, Oregon. We're working together to figure out how to strengthen the rooftops of gigantic warehouses so we can tap that vast underutilized space. There are millions of buildings that could create their own electricity and sell the excess back to the grid as well, but we need to be able to fortify the existing structures to hold the excess weight."

"That's an expensive proposition—converting existing commercial warehouses to hold the additional weight."

"The main issue is to develop the steam technology. Then, even if we can't modify existing structures, we can build new construction that is strong enough in the first place. That, or place the technology on the ground or anywhere with good sun exposure. The structure of such a power plant can always be designed."

"This is all very interesting," he finally said. "I'll talk with my two architect friends who are alternative energy gurus, and I'll get back with you."

Two months went by. Every time I would call North Carolina and ask about joining us at least financially, the answer was, "We are thinking about it" or "We are working on it."

During one of our calls, I mentioned I was going to Denver to check in on my building, which was, as yet, unsold.

"What do you have there?" he asked.

As he asked me a few more questions about the property, I could tell he was surprised I owned a large building. All of a sudden, I was not just somebody with a vague idea, but, as I had hoped, a business-man with a substantial commercial investment.

Four days later when we chatted again, he said, "Listen, John, I like your idea, but it'll require money."

"Yes," I admitted.

"I am sending you $500,000. See what you can do with it."

I was elated. The cash infusion would give me the ability to hire some brainpower and ferret out the necessary science. It was going to take a lot more than that, but the money meant legitimate oppor-tunity. "That's incredible. Thank you."

"Tell me a little more about your building in Denver."

I provided all the details including that I had it listed with Coldwell Banker.

"How many tenants do you have?"

"None. It is a one-tenant building. I don't want to break it up to have a lot of tenants because I want to work on my current business venture, not be a landlord."

We finished our call with his promise that a business proposal, check, and necessary paperwork were in the mail.

A week went by.

Then two.

I called him four weeks later to find out where things were.

"John, I have a better idea."

Oh no, I thought. *Here it comes . . .*

"I really want this solar energy project of yours to succeed," he said. "But if I put a lot of money on the line and organize the brain-power, as you put it, I need some security."

"As in?"

"We both know the real estate market is terrible. You may not lease your property in Denver for three to four years. You may lose it. What if we were to form a three-way partnership on your building? One third you, one third your current partner, and one third me? I can refinance the property with a company where I have a track record."

"I'm listening," I said.

"The two architects here in Raleigh are on board. They have, and we have, connections to all manner of experts like Dr. Wilson in the physics department at the University of Chicago. They also have an Alternative Energy department there. In addition, I have connections to financial heavy hitters. We'll sell them shares in SPI."

As I listened, he added, "One thing that you need to do is move to Denver and lease the property. Once you are there, you can contact the National Renewable Energy Laboratory.

"I've spoken with them already, and they are interested to hear more."

"You see what I mean. I believe it's a hell of a business plan."

We were a start-up company that hadn't even started up. If I thought of all the engineers, scientists, and different tradespeople I needed to locate and then pay for their services, it would cost several million dollars before we ever had a product. The more I thought about it, the more workable the deal sounded. I was in for two-thirds of my Denver property, which I acquired for a couple hundred thousand dollars. However, the building was going to be financed and paid for by the new entity, which would be three of us, 33.33 % each.

Over the next few weeks, we formed an independent Colorado LLC. I named it TMC Partnership, LLC. It was a three-way partnership with the stipulation that Solar Power International (a separate entity) could use the building to generate cash if need be. SPI would be operated from North Carolina because we could have an office and staff, at no cost. In addition, there was easy access to people who were well versed in alternative energy. They also had labor at their disposal until SPI was generating money.

When I outlined the terms of the deal to a legal advisor he said, "John, you have a beautiful commercial property that cost you some two hundred thousand down to purchase. You have a year or so to finance it and pay off the sellers. But the economy is bad. What if you cannot lease it? How are you going to pay that tremendous monthly payment to keep the building? Instead, you've added a strong partner. What they are offering you is the chance to finance your dreams.

ROCKY MOUNTAIN HIGH

I moved to Denver and was happy to be there. I love the Rocky Mountains, loved to ski, and had grown tired of Southern California—the politics were a disaster, there were too many people, and the smog and traffic were atrocious.

The first thing I did was visit the Air Force Academy in Colorado Springs. For me, as a refugee from behind the Iron Curtain, I found it unforgettable to be allowed to roam freely on the campus. In some ways, it was the true definition of freedom.

My mission in Denver was to get the building leased as soon as possible. Since the building was originally mine, and I had experience and a broker's license, who better to handle the transaction than me?

The first thing I did was set up an office in the main reception area. I put in a phone and placed my electric typewriter on the desk. Then, I purchased a sleeping bag because I planned to stay in the building until I learned everything about the surroundings. It was 1993 and business was starting to develop in the Montbello area, but it was generally considered to be a depressed area with a lot of unemployment. Not to mention gang problems. At the time, there were two motels, a McDonald's, a gas station, a bank, and the Montbello Tech Facility (as I had named it). I quickly realized why the insurance company had been anxious to sell the building, and why the Coldwell Banker brokers were not able to create any interest in the building. They probably didn't even try, given the location.

However, the area was set up for future profitability because it was located right by the I-70 exit for the new airport which was under construction. In other words, it had three things going for it: location, location, location.

Still, several months went by with no takers. Everyone suggested I break up the building to a multi-tenant capacity, but I did not want to do that. It would cost a lot of money, and I was doing well by setting up short-term leases. I rented some of the space in the building to small tenants who were suppliers of the new airport project. One of them was a food catering outfit who was going to be a permanent resident at the airport. They rented one third of the building and they paid better than market price.

They were there for over a year.

One day, a gentleman walked into my office and introduced himself as John Smith, publisher of the *Greater Far Northeast Reporter*, the community newspaper for the Montbello area. John Smith was something of the self-appointed mayor of Montbello. He was like an ombudsman, and got behind my efforts to successfully lease the building.

"It will put Montbello on the map," he said.

He interviewed me about the building and did what turned out to be a full front-page interview entitled, "From High Tech to Super Tech: Dignity, Pride, And Diversity."

I was proud of my building and the article he wrote that high-lighted it.

One day a gentleman walked into my office representing a large Canadian gift and novelty company. They were getting ready to ca-ter a major event taking place in Denver and needed a lot of secure warehouse space—around 35,000 square feet.

"What is the event?"

"World Youth Day, which is actually a week-long event in Denver organized by the Catholic church. It is an arrangement between the Vatican and the American Archbishops. The Pope will be in atten-dance, as will President Clinton."

I was delighted when they rented half the building and moved in a month before the event. They had thousands of gift items, all with the Pope's picture on them—everything from beach towels to coffee mugs. When the event was over, the company stayed for a year, sell-ing their inventory to Catholic schools across the U.S.

Still, I did not have a long-term tenant for the Montbello Tech Facility. I decided I would speak with the mayor of Denver, knowing if a large corporation wanted to relocate, they were more than likely to call the mayor's office for suggestions and tax incentives. In my mind, a company that large would be smart to settle close to the new airport.

I went down to city hall without an appointment and was prompt-ly turned away by security. As I was leaving, I saw another security officer and asked him, "How can you see the mayor in his office?"

"That's easy. He has an open door policy on Wednesdays. Come then, and they will let you in to see him and speak with him."

I was there at ten o'clock the following Wednesday. Wellington Webb, a tall, pleasant man, who always wore tennis shoes, was the mayor at the time. His door was, in fact, open.

The guard looked at my identification and let me in.

The mayor offered me a seat and I told him the story about Montbello Tech—that it had been a long time, but I was trying to lease it, and it was a one-tenant building. I said I knew it was not a good economy, but the community of Montbello needed an employer who could possibly hire 1000 people.

"Is there anything you can do to help me lease the property?" I went on to ask. "It will certainly help me as an owner, but I am also thinking of the unemployed people of Montbello."

"I know Montbello, and I know John Smith well," Mayor Webb said about the newspaper publisher. "The airport is coming along. I have no doubt that someone will be interested in leasing that space long-term in the near future."

"Mr. Mayor, I thank you for seeing me, and if an opportunity comes along, please let me know," I said.

"I certainly will. Thank you for your concern for the people of Montbello, and say hello to John Smith for me."

A few months went by.

One afternoon, a bus pulled up right near the door. To my surprise, thirty people piled out and entered the building. They were led by Mayor Webb, tennis shoes and all.

"Hi John," he said remembering my name. "I took these people to the airport project for an official visit. We were on the way back, and I thought we'd stop by and walkthrough and let them see your building."

"By all means," I said and guided the delegation through, explaining and answering questions as I went.

When it was over, Mr. Webb said thank you and wished me well. With that, they all piled back on the bus and left.

About three or four months later, six people came through my door. The lady in charge said they were from the real estate division of the U.S. Postal Service. I gathered my wits and led them through the building. They seemed to like all I presented to them. So much so in fact, she said, "I will call you back by noon tomorrow and more than likely will give you a proposal to lease the building."

I barely slept that night.

As promised, they were all in my office the next day. They handed me the proposal and said, "We would like an answer in seven days. If you accept our offer, we'll get our attorneys together with your attorneys and let them work out a deal between you and the United States Postal Service. If we have an agreement, then we'll want to completely gut the building and rebuild the inside according to U.S. Postal design. The rebuild will be over and above the lease price."

Since my partners were contractors, we were able to make a deal and manage the construction.

I asked Mayor Webb twice whether he'd been instrumental in getting us the U.S. Postal Service as a tenant. He said no, but I do believe he was somehow involved.

When the project was finished, the building was used as a telecall center for eleven western states. When a postal customer wanted information from their local post office, they were actually speaking with someone in my building. I found that out personally when I called what I thought was my post office in Pacific Palisades, California to cancel my P.O. box and learned I was speaking to someone in my very own building.

After the USPS lease was over, the building was sold to the city of Denver for over eight million dollars. Not bad for a two hundred thousand dollar investment. TMC Partnership made money with the lease and about 7.8 million through the sale of the property, allowing me to realize my dream of creating a multi-million-dollar, concentrated solar power company.

SOLAR POWER INTERNATIONAL

Solar Power International, a seemingly impossible dream to make steam out of the sun's energy, was evolving to do just that.

We partnered with the University of Chicago physics department. (The same department that could split the nucleus of an atom during World War II, six months before the Germans did so with two scientists of Hungarian origin at the vanguard: Szilard Leo and Ede Teller.) The university had experimented with solar energy since the early 1950s under the leadership of Professor Roland Winston; they had many experiences and much scientific knowledge we could respect and use.

By forming a strong relationship with us, they had a commercial partner who brought business know-how to their research. As we progressed, we formed other subsidiaries, and brought in various other associates, partners, and a number of big investors.

We named one subsidiary Solar Roof International. The first product the company came up with used optics to concentrate the sun's energy onto a pipe to heat up a liquid that would circulate for floor heating. Eventually, the liquid would run an air conditioning unit or provide heat to a building.

The first project we got was a 10,000 square footprint shop in California. I personally worked to install that system on the roof along with several of our engineers and executives.

We designed a two-story building in North Carolina with a heavy steel structure to enable it to generate its own electricity atop the building and take the entire building off grid. Later, we built a 30,000 square foot "Day Light" building for a corporation in South Carolina. It was designed to not only generate its own electricity, but so lights never needed to be turned on in the building during the day.

We not only installed one of our systems in a New York skyscraper, but we got a $5,000,0000 contract from Mayor Daly for senior homes, jails, and schools owned by the city of Chicago. Mayor Daly offered us a somewhat dilapidated brick building to assemble the equipment free of rent. We had to rehab the building, but we were able to create a manufacturing facility in Chicago to produce rooftop hot water panels that could be used for hot water, heat swimming pools, and heating systems in general.

We had an invitation from Duke Energy in North Carolina to create a joint venture with them; the company would be called Duke Solar. Duke Energy was the ninth largest electric company in the world. They built power plants all over the globe, but always retained a certain percent ownership of them. We jumped on the offer, the idea being that we could go around the world to build projects with Duke Energy, who had first-class engineering expertise and the funds to make it all happen. Unfortunately, Duke Energy reneged on the joint venture agreement because the board of directors changed. Thankfully, we did not just walk away from the deal with them—it cost Duke some millions.

In the meantime, we did not stop progressing toward steam. The National Renewable Energy Laboratory, which is part of the U.S. Department of Energy and located in Denver, Colorado, helped us a great deal. At that time they had nearly 1,000 engineers working on renewable technologies. They liked what we were trying to do with our technology and wanted to help us. NREL built us a 30 x 20 platform outside of Albuquerque, New Mexico that could turn left and right and up or down on which we could install a segment of our newly designed solar section. About forty feet away, there was a temporary structure full of computers and three engineers who monitored all of the data from our solar section on the platform. I was amongst the people from our company who manned the platform and performed various systematic experiments.

Our system worked beautifully.

We discovered that on a clear night when the moon was shining, we could generate energy as well. The data we collected was very valuable to our company and went a long way for us to be able to create steam.

The best part was we never got a bill from NREL for their effort to help us.

I later learned the Israelis and the French were experimenting too. There was a company in France that created a water tower with close to a million mirrors surrounding and aimed at the water tower container. They were able to make extremely hot water, but not steam—not at that time.

The government began to pressure power plants across the USA to get involved with energy sources beyond coal, oil, and gas. As a result, we were able to build several one-, two-, and three-megawatt plants, using what is called Concentrated Solar Power Technology. They were forerunners of the big plant. We finally had an opportunity to build in Nevada through a company we named Solargenix.

We looked at land located near Boulder City, around 32 miles from Las Vegas in the Eldorado Valley, which was close to a large transmission line where we could put the generated electricity. To begin work, we faced a lot of environmental demonstrations from different organizations—mostly to protect desert frogs and lizards that lived in that area. Because we were helping to alleviate the need for fossil fuels, which hurt millions of people and animals on the planet, we eventually prevailed.

We started construction on Nevada Solar One CSP, the largest solar power plant worldwide in nearly twenty years, and what would become the third biggest alternative energy power plant in the world. Nevada Solar One was spread over an area of 400 acres, 300 acres of which would be in use. This approximately equaled the dimensions of 200 soccer fields. It was constructed of 760 parabolic trough concentrating solar collectors, which constitute 182,000 curved mirrors sitting on a structure of seven million pounds of recycled aluminum. Driven by computer, the rows of concentrating solar collectors precisely follow the rays of the sun to produce 64 megawatts and 129,000,000 kwh of electricity per year—enough to supply 20,000 households per year. The whole energy production of Nevada Solar One was sold to Nevada Power Company and the Sierra Pacific Resources.

The technology was unlike anything ever used before: mirrors that concentrated sunlight onto a steel absorber tube with a special black coating to heat it quickly inside a vacuum space created by a glass tube that surrounds the black absorber tube. A special fluid flows inside this black tube, which heats up to 750° F or 400° C. This hot, synthetic fluid was pumped to a heat exchanger where it turns water into steam, which, in turn, drives a steam turbine to produce electricity. The steam cools as it turns the turbine, becomes liquid water again, and is then reheated again by the solar collectors in a repeating cycle. The electricity created would then be distributed among five different states, although most would go to Las Vegas.

According to a report from the U.S. Department of Energy, and published through the National Renewable Energy Laboratory, the parabolic technology used in Nevada Solar One, represented the most successful results of alternative energy production and stated the technology would soon compete with conventional oil, coal, and gas technologies.

Nevada Solar Power was completed for $248,000,000, financed in large part by a Spanish energy company. It became operational on June 27, 2007. We sold the power to Nevada Power, put it into their high wires, and they distributed it at a lifetime rate of twenty cents per kilowatt.

The dedication took place on February 22, 2008, and was attended by 400, including scientists, engineers, conservationists, federal and state politicians, businessmen, and entrepreneurs, astronaut Dr. Sally Ride, and Apple co-founder Steve Wozniak. The master of ceremonies was environmentalist and actor Ed Begley Jr. Art Linkletter, who was one of the directors of Solargenix Energy, was 95 years old and could not attend the ceremony due to illness.

We rented a big tent, which we set up beside the first row of mirrors so the guests could see them up close. The mirrors were turned face down toward the ground until we began the ceremony with the music from *2001: A Space Odyssey*. At that moment, the row of 26-foot-long mirrors started to turn in time with the music. It was so dramatic that many people in the audience teared up.

I was no exception.

When the song ended and the mirrors turned completely up, there was a standing ovation in the middle of the Nevada desert.

Today, a number of companies continue to experiment with and develop solar energy including the Spanish company we partnered with for Nevada Solar Power, which is in the process of constructing a 200-megawatt facility in one of the Arab countries. Using the rays of the sun, many companies produce steam for energy production all around the world. Whole buildings are being constructed that are entirely energy self-sufficient. Old buildings are being retrofitted to accommodate such energy production.

To this day, Nevada Solar One reduces carbon dioxide emissions into the environment by 280 million pounds or about 129 million kilograms, the equivalent of removing 20,000 cars from the roads.

I am very proud to call this my greatest professional accomplishment.

LIVING THE DREAM

If I've learned one lesson in life it is this: Never be so proud you are unwilling to make a 180 degree turn. Once, I had to do just that when I found myself facing the giant propellors of a KC 135 in a Cessna 150. That day, changing course quickly literally saved my life. I've done the same thing figuratively, in countless ways, throughout my eighty-plus years.

As a boy, I wanted to be many things—a railroad man, pilot, soldier, engineer, actor, and entrepreneur. While I did have a menial job on the rails for a time, none of my other goals were possible while I was trapped behind the Iron Curtain. In fact, my future seemed destined to include imprisonment or worse, simply because I believed in capitalism and freedom.

It never ceases to amaze me that most conflict in the world— fighting, killing, and world wars— have been caused by religion, political dogma, and people who think they can be or should be called God.

Maybe it's because my family survived some of the worst humankind has to offer, but I have learned if you keep your wits about you, eventually a solution presents itself to every challenge. It is an attitude I maintained when I was forced to flee my family, friends, and the only life I'd ever known in Hungary, the spirit I brought with me to America as a refugee, and part of my resolve to be a successful student, actor, businessman, and entrepreneur.

Along the way, there were people who doubted whether what I was trying to do was right or even possible. There were also those who tried to undermine me by trying to take credit for something I thought of, created, or implemented. As a result, I was forced to consider every situation in light of winning the particular battle or the war itself. I learned over the years, and as a result of my many experiences, to follow former President Ronald Reagan's golden rule: Trust but verify. In the end, there is nothing as satisfying as overcoming a problem to achieve a goal. Especially when that goal is the American Dream.

I would like to be remembered as an entrepreneur, innovator, actor, writer, producer, aviator, sailor, and skier. In America, I was afforded great opportunities: a scholarship to college, acting roles, the freedom to be an inventor and entrepreneur, and even the ability to enjoy such pleasures as owning a boat, ski racing, and attaining my pilot's license. I enjoyed the blessing of being a parent and grandparent and the joys of business success. I even reached my lifelong goal of investing in and executive producing two films: *Saint John of Las Vegas* and *Badassdom*.

Along the way, there have been uniquely American moments I count as true highlights including my 1973 commission as a Kentucky Colonel by Governor Wendell H. Ford for charity work. In my boyhood, I could never have imagined my 1978 adoption into the Sioux American Nation by Iron Eyes Cody where I was given the name Thanka Wanbli or Big Eagle.

When I left Hungary in 1956, I told my high school buddies I would never forget them, unsure whether I'd ever be able to return, much less see my family or friends again. One thing I never expected was to be able to return annually for the last thirty years. Not only have I been able to reunite and reconnect with my relatives and friends but experience and enjoy a free Hungary.

In 1998, I successfully guided a hot air balloon named Mistral over Hungarian skies and was given the name, per tradition, of Gróf Sámsondombossy or Count Sámsondombossy. In 2000, my old high school friends and I got together to commission and unveil a statue and flagpole in the schoolyard at our old alma mater, the Bookkeeping Technical High School. A bronze plaque at the base bears the names of our class.

Every year, when I return, my friends and I get together and celebrate our friendship with big parties. On one of my annual trips, and one of those parties with my best buddies whom my mother affectionately called the Gang of Árpad Square, they told me they wanted to introduce me to a particular lady.

"She is beautiful, she's got a nice figure, and she can cook," they said.

A meeting was set up for the next day at a corner on the main street of town in front of the movie house and close to a restaurant—painfully close to the site where I was arrested by the police when I returned to Hungary for the first time as a U.S. citizen. Because I was set to meet a woman whom my friends described as the most beautiful lady in Debrecen, I didn't say a word to my friend Laci who came along to make the introduction.

Suddenly, there Erzsbet was—beautiful with a charming smile and gorgeous eyes. She was even more lovely than my friends and their wives had promised.

The introduction happened, my friend disappeared, and off we went to a nearby restaurant for dinner.

Twenty five year later, we are still an item. I see Erzsbet, whom I affectionately call Elizabeth, every year. I am in Hungary for three months and she joins me here in the United States for six months every year. She was with me when my sister Irén Czingula Szekerákné died in September of 2011 and has been my companion on a number of incredible trips including Crete, Santorini, Mexico, and a two-month RV trip to see the western United States. We've been all over Europe including the Hapsburg Castles, the Hapsburg Ball in Vienna, Wagner's Opera House in Bavaria, and Franc Liszt's residence. We've even gone to the South Pacific Islands including Tahiti, Moorea, and Bora Bora.

When I was young, I wanted to buy a sailboat and sail around the world on my own. I owned a two-engine motorboat in Los Angeles, but I never came close to reaching my goal until Erzsbet and I boarded the Cunard Line for the maiden voyage of the 3rd Queen Elizabeth. I spent three and a half blissful months with my Queen Elizabeth Tóth on the trip of a lifetime around the world. I've been so lucky to find her, however late in life.

Like my American army jacket with the Hungarian Revolutionary emblem, I treasure the connections, people, and experiences that have allowed me to live my Hungarian American dream.